TO LIVE
LIKE A TREE
ALONE AND FREE
LIKE A FOREST
IN BROTHERHOOD

Organized by

Founded in 1987, **American Turkish Association of North Carolina (ATA-NC)** is a non-profit, member supported organization dedicated to promoting awareness of Turkish culture and sharing Turkish heritage throughout the state of North Carolina.

Sponsored By

The 2011 Nazim Hikmet Poetry Festival has been made possible by a major grant from the Turkish Cultural Foundation (www.turkishculturalfoundation.org)

Hosted & Sponsored by

| TOWN Of CARY | Parks, Recreation & Cultural Resources | www.townofcary.org |

Support also provided by

www.sistercitiesofcary.org

Organizing Committee
Buket Aydemir, Pelin Balı, Mehmet C. Öztürk, Birgül Tuzlalı

Cover Design: Pelin Balı
Copyright: American Turkish Association of North Carolina

A chapbook of talks and poetry

Fourth Annual
Nâzım Hikmet Poetry Festival

April 15, 2012 • Page Walker Arts & History Center • Cary, NC

Table of Contents

Preface 6

Nâzım Hikmet - Biography 8

Pablo Neruda - Biography 12

Invited Talks
   From Neruda to Neruda: My journey toward the poet and his poetry -
   Carlos Trujillo 14
   Neruda's Irreverent Elegies - Greg Dawes 24

Poetry Competition
   Selection Committee 36

   Finalists:
     Hala Alyan 43
     Peter Blair 50
     Kevin Boyle 56
     Amy Leigh Brown 60
     Hedy Habra 66
     Jeffrey Kahrs 72
     Daniel Abdal-Hayy Moore 76
     Anna Lena Phillips 84
     Iris Tillman 88
     Tim VanDyke 94

   Honorable Mentions
     Elizabeth Gargano 102
     Emily Romeyn 108

Previous Festivals 113

Preface

The Nâzım Hikmet Poetry Festival brings together poets, scholars and the community in a one-day annual event celebrating poetry and honoring the Turkish poet Nâzım Hikmet. The festival has become a major forum for cultural exchange and a mainstay of the local and global cultural landscape.

The focus of the 2012 Fourth Annual Nâzım Hikmet Poetry Festival is the Chilean poet Pablo Neruda and his poetry. Professors Carlos Trujillo of Villanova University and Greg Dawes of NC State University were invited to speak, and we are indebted to both for their papers, included in this chapbook. Dr. Trujillo was not able to join us today due to a family health emergency. We are grateful to his colleague and friend Agustin Pasten for joining us to read his paper.

The heart of the festival is a competition open to poets around the world. The selection committee for 2012 included Greg Dawes, Joe Donahue, Dorianne Laux, Murat Nemet-Nejat, Tanya Olson and Hatice Örün Öztürk. Preliminary judging was done by Dianne Timblin. We are grateful for their conscientious and magnanimous work.

This year's competition received over 700 submissions from 250 poets. North Carolina poets submitted 53% of the poems. The remainder came from the rest of the United States (29%) and other countries (18%). Dianne Timblin's reading winnowed the field to 120 poets, from which the selection committee chose ten winners and two honorable mentions. These twelve poets are now members of the Hikmet family; they are the strength of our 2012 festival. We are happy to have once more among our finalists published poets with previous awards as well as rising poets winning their first prizes.

All twelve finalists were invited to read their poems at the festival. Four of the finalists, who were unable to come to the festival sent their videos. We were also happy to have two out-of state poets, Daniel Abdel-Hayy Moore from Philadelphia and Jeffrey Kahrs from Seattle with us.

We had two second-time winners this year: Kevin Boyle and Daniel Abdel-Hayy Moore were among the finalists of the 2011 competition.

Our invited poet was Joseph Millar, winner of many prestigious awards and fellowships including the 2008 Pushcart prize and the 2012 Guggenheim fellowship. CJ Suitt, co-director of Sacrificial Poets also joined the festival to read several of his poems. Our festival is graced by their participation. In addition, Celisa Steele, Claudine Moreau and David Manning, award winning poets of the North Carolina Poetry Society (NCPS) were among us with their poems. Celisa Steele was among the finalists of the 2010 Nazim Hikmet Poetry Competition. We are grateful to them and NCPS for their participation.

The 2012 festival included two workshops, an adult workshop for ages 15 and up given by Alice Osborn and a youth workshop led by Michael Beadle for ages 11 to 14. We are grateful to both Alice and Michael for their efforts.

We would also like to thank Semih Poroy, the renowned Turkish cartoonist, for the use of his portrait of Nâzım Hikmet. Mr. Poroy is known internationally for his political cartoons, many commenting on current affairs and championing free speech.

This year's festival was again made possible by a major grant from the Turkish Cultural Foundation. We would like to extend our gratitude to TCF and especially to Ms. Güler Köknar, executive director of the Foundation, for her continued support. The Town of Cary (Dept. of Parks, Recreation and Cultural Recourses) also provided precious funding as well as the venue, the Page Walker Arts & History Center, a poetic setting appropriate to our festival. Special thanks go to Mayor Harold Weinbrecht, Mr. Lyman Collins, and Mrs. Kris Carmichael for their encouragement and support. Due to the generosity of the TCF and the Town of Cary, we are able to open our doors to general public free of charge and invite our guests. Additionally, we express our sincere appreciation to Sister Cities of Cary Association for their help in reaching the community.

Last but not least, we are grateful to all the friends whose volunteer efforts made the festival and this chapbook possible.

April 2012

Buket Aydemir, Pelin Balı, Mehmet C. Öztürk, Birgül Tuzlalı
Fourth Annual Nâzım Hikmet Poetry Festival Organizing Committee

Nâzım Hikmet

Nâzım Hikmet, the foremost modern Turkish poet, was born in 1902 in Selânik. He grew up in Istanbul and was introduced to poetry early, publishing his first poems at the age of 17. He attended the Naval Academy but was discharged due to repeated bouts of pleurisy. Attracted by the Russian revolution and its promise of social justice, he crossed the border and made his way to Moscow and studied Political Science and Economics. He met the poet Vladimir Mayakovsky and other artists of the futurist movement and his style changed from Ottoman literary conventions to free verse.

He returned to Turkey in 1928 and spent five of the next ten years in prison on a variety of trumped-up charges due to his leftist views. During this time, he published nine books that revolutionized Turkish poetry and the Turkish language.

In 1938, he was arrested for supposedly inciting the Turkish armed forces to revolt. He was sentenced to 28 years in prison on the grounds that military cadets were reading his poems. While in prison, he composed some of his greatest poems as well as his epic masterpiece *Human Landscapes from My Country*. He wrote a total of 66,000 lines; according to his letters, 17,000 of those survived.

In 1949, an international committee including Pablo Picasso, Paul Robeson and Jean Paul Sartre was formed in Paris to campaign for his release. In 1950 he was awarded the World Peace Prize, which Pablo Neruda accepted on his behalf. The same year he went on an 18-day hunger strike despite a recent heart attack and was released under the general amnesty of the newly elected government. Following his release, there were repeated attempts to murder him. He was followed everywhere. When he was ordered to do his military service at the age of fifty, he fled the country and was stripped of Turkish citizenship. His citizenship was officially restored by the Turkish government fifty-eight years later on January 5, 2009.

Nâzım Hikmet did not live to see his later poems published in Turkish, although they were translated into more than forty languages during his lifetime. He died of a heart attack in 1963, at the age of sixty-one. During the fifteen years after his death, his eight volume "Collected Poems", plays, novels and letters were gradually published.

Many celebrations of Nazim's 100th birthday took place in 2002: the Turkish Ministry of Culture sponsored several events; UNESCO named 2002 "The Year of Nâzım Hikmet"; and the American Poetry Review put him on their cover and published a collection of his poems.

Pablo Neruda and Nâzım Hikmet together at Alexander Pushkin's 150th birthday celebration.

Honoring Pablo Neruda

Pablo Neruda (1904-1973), whose real name is Neftalí Ricardo Reyes Basoalto, was born on 12 July, 1904, in the town of Parral in Chile. His father was a railway employee and his mother, who died shortly after his birth, a teacher. Some years later his father, who had then moved to the town of Temuco, remarried doña Trinidad Candia Malverde. The poet spent his childhood and youth in Temuco, where he also got to know Gabriela Mistral, head of the girls' secondary school, who took a liking to him. At the early age of thirteen he began to contribute some articles to the daily "La Mañana", among them, "Entusiasmo y Perseverancia" - his first publication - and his first poem. In 1920, he became a contributor to the literary journal *Selva Austral* under the pen name of Pablo Neruda, which he adopted in memory of the Czechoslovak poet Jan Neruda (1834-1891). Some of the poems Neruda wrote at that time are to be found in his first published book: *Crepusculario* (1923). The following year saw the publication of *Veinte poemas de amor y una cancion desesperada*, one of his best-known and most translated works. Alongside his literary activities, Neruda studied French and pedagogy at the University of Chile in Santiago.

Between 1927 and 1935, the government put him in charge of a number of honorary consulships, which took him to Burma, Ceylon, Java, Singapore, Buenos Aires, Barcelona, and Madrid. His poetic production during that difficult period included, among other works, the collection of esoteric surrealistic poems, *Residencia en la tierra* (1933), which marked his literary breakthrough.

The Spanish Civil War and the murder of García Lorca, whom Neruda knew, affected him strongly and made him join the Republican movement, first in Spain, and later in France, where he started working on his collection of poems *España en el Corazón* (1937). The same year he returned to his native country, to which he had been recalled, and his poetry during the following period was characterised by an orientation towards political and social matters. *España en el Corazón* had a great impact by virtue of its being printed in the middle of the front during the civil war.

In 1939, Neruda was appointed consul for the Spanish emigration, residing in Paris, and, shortly afterwards, Consul General in Mexico, where he rewrote his *Canto General de Chile*, transforming it into an epic poem about the whole South American continent, its nature, its people and its historical destiny. This work, entitled *Canto General*, was published in Mexico 1950, and also underground in Chile. It consists of approximately 250 poems brought together into fifteen literary cycles and constitutes the central part of Neruda's production. Shortly after its publication, *Canto General* was translated into some ten languages. Nearly all these poems were created in a difficult situation, when Neruda was living abroad.

In 1943, Neruda returned to Chile, and in 1945 he was elected senator of the Republic, also joining the Communist Party of Chile. Due to his protests against President González Videla's repressive policy against striking miners in 1947, he had to live underground in his own country for two years until he managed to leave in 1949. After living in different European countries he returned home in 1952. A great deal of what he published during that period bears the stamp of his political activities; one example is *Las Uvas y el Viento* (1954), which can be regarded as the diary of Neruda's exile. In *Odas elementales* (1954- 1959) his message is expanded into a more extensive description of the world, where the objects of the hymns - things, events and relations - are duly presented in alphabetic form.

Neruda's production is exceptionally extensive. For example, his *Obras Completas*, constantly republished, comprised 459 pages in 1951; in 1962 the number of pages was 1,925, and in 1968 it amounted to 3,237, in two volumes. Among his works of the last few years can be mentioned *Cien sonetos de amor* (1959), which includes poems dedicated to his wife Matilde Urrutia, *Memorial de Isla Negra*, a poetic work of an autobiographic character in five volumes, published on the occasion of his sixtieth birthday, *Arte de pajáros* (1966), *La Barcarola* (1967), *the play Fulgor y muerte de Joaquín Murieta* (1967), *Las manos del día* (1968), *Fin del mundo* (1969), *Las piedras del cielo* (1970), and *La espada encendida*.

"Pablo Neruda - Biography". Nobelprize.org. 5 Apr 2012 http://www.nobelprize.org/nobel_prizes/literature/laureates/1971/neruda.html

From Neruda to Neruda:
My journey toward the poet and his poetry

Carlos Trujillo
Villanova University

Like every Chilean child of the 1950s I probably heard Neruda's name many times whether it was in school or at home since I had three older sisters and two of them were in high school. So certainly as a toddler I probably heard that name and perhaps some of his most famous poems known throughout the country beginning with the publication of his second book in 1924, *Twenty Love Poems and a Song of Despair*.

I probably heard his name but I should also point out that during my first ten years of life I didn't read any of Neruda's work since the only books we had in my house were very old and worn out copies of the Old Testament and the New Testament. Sure, I definitely read those books every day since they were the only reading material that we had at home since my parents had been born in the countryside and had lived there for most of their lives. Certainly the sensuality of the love poetry in Neruda's first two books probably wasn't present in the readings in elementary school, but the name of the poet must have come to me quickly from somewhere because the day that I saw Pablo Neruda, and for some reason I am not sure how it became a part of my memory, I already knew who that illustrious figure was.

On one of those many Saturday mornings that my father took me to the beach to buy fish and seafood, we went up Calle Blanco, like we usually did, but one block before the Plaza de Armas we turned right to see why a large crowd had gathered at the entrance of the Cine Rex Theater. Such large and happy crowds were somewhat uncommon in my town, even more so on a Saturday morning. So I probably asked my father if we could stop by to see what was happening. I don't remember ever having entered the theater previously so the mere possibility of going into that building pulled at me like a magnet. When we arrived at the theater – filled with people – I asked him if I could have a quick look and with the tenderness of any father faced with such a small wish of a child, he let me do it.

If he knew the cause for such joy, my father didn't tell me or I can't simply remember if he told me because that little detail didn't contribute anything to my fond memory of that morning. The seats in the orchestra section of the theater were probably full and the doors were probably already closed because I went up by the stairs that faced the gallery and the balcony (sections that we called the peanut gallery) and suddenly I found myself in the middle of a crazy crowd. Nervous and shocked in the middle of a crowd of people whom I didn't know, and somewhat confused, I stopped in the middle of the center aisle just as someone was introducing the person who was the reason behind the gathering of the large crowd. Amidst cheers and applause the poet Pablo Neruda appeared near the front of the stage and he began to talk with that famously nasal voice that over the years and with his increasing recognition around the world became so beloved and unmistakable for the majority of my compatriots.

What did he say? What was he talking about? I don't know but that doesn't really matter in this story. What was truly the most important and magical part of that Saturday morning is that a shy young boy who had never entered the Cine Rex before because he didn't have enough money and because going to the movies wasn't a necessity for a family who had just moved from the countryside a few years earlier, had entered such an attractive and unfamiliar place without paying and suddenly found himself face to face with the poet Pablo Neruda (in reality, about 20 to 30 meters, that is, 65 to 100 feet), who surely had come to Castro in order to collaborate on a political campaign. And that was it! I saw Neruda, I listened to Neruda and I always remembered the image of Neruda cheered by everyone and of his nasal voice saying things that I probably didn't understand nor try to understand. That literary figure and that voice remained engraved in my memory for the rest of my life.

Years passed, the readings began, and after the Bible my sisters' textbooks followed. My favorite books were the anthologies that they used in their Spanish-language classes. The yellowish pages in the hefty hardcover volumes were a marvelous world, which I joyfully entered each time my sisters left them on top of the kitchen table. The joy and wonderment combined in the reading of the pages of those old books that contained beautiful poetry written in Spanish. But, these were anthologies of Spanish Poetry, that is, written by poets from Spain, so there wasn't even a trace of Neruda in them. So, the poems of my famous compatriot would have to wait.

As a high school student I remember many of the required readings. But those that I really remember the most were those readings that I chose to read on my own and to which I devoted each hour of free time that we had in high school when I found a quiet area in the school library. When I arrived there the librarian already knew what I was going to ask for: any volume of *The Treasury of Children's Literature*. On those pages I began my journey around the world and, especially the world of Greek and Roman mythology, which was what had interested me the most. Therefore, it wasn't surprising that once I graduated with the degree of Teacher of Spanish, one of my first purchases was specifically to buy that marvelous volume contained in the very same collection that I had read in my free time in my high school library.

So where does Neruda fit into all of this? The truth is that I don't have any memory of having had one of his books of poetry when I was a high school student, though of course, I remember reading and knowing about a few of his poems. But I just don't remember if I had ever even held any of Neruda's books in my own hands. Nevertheless, I knew about the figure of the poet and I learned new things about him every day. Pablo Neruda was a well-known literary figure throughout my country, and as such, he was indisputable and unavoidable.

In 1969 I left the island of Chiloé to begin my university studies and as fate would have it, this shy young student would buy tickets to go to Temuco, the city of Neruda's childhood and adolescence. I would remain there for five years completing my studies at the local campus of the University of Chile, getting acquainted with the forests and rainfall which were reminiscent of my island but with less rain. A few years before I began my university studies in Temuco I wrote poetry (or in reality, I put some words together on paper), but nothing would compare to what happened to me when I arrived in Temuco. I became even more shy and introverted and for a number of reasons: the distance between my home and Temuco, the differences in my new world and my new surroundings, the need for my parents and my family, and finding myself far away from my friends, my neighborhood, and my usual routine. But I was beginning to study literature and those always endearing books that filled those bookshelves of the university's library, I began to love even more and more. Poetry flowed like an important river at the end of the 60s and the beginning of the 70s, and at the same time that my youthfulness overwhelmed me and left me bogged down with doubts and questions. The political fighting made its mark in Chilean society in August and the parliamentary elections that would be held in March would in some way allow the political parties to size each other up in anticipation of the presidential election that would occur the following year.

Regardless, my arrival in Temuco coincided with a greater closeness to poetry or Temuco was the reason that poetry became an essential part of my life. Since I had begun my studies at the University writing became my daily bread, a real, urgent, and basic need. Nevertheless, I didn't dare show my poems to anyone, and I didn't even tell anyone that I was writing poetry. Poetry was a personal matter, an intimate secret that I couldn't share with anyone. But it was not a matter of keeping it a secret because I thought that I was so good at writing poetry but rather it was purely and exclusively because my shyness would not let me do it and added to this shyness was my fear that my critics would have concluded that my poems weren't worthwhile. To make matters worse, shortly after beginning my classes I found out that three of my classmates – all of them from the land of Neruda – were poets or they thought they were poets. None of them thought much of each other's poetry, and they criticized the importance of each other's work. Such a discovery led me to promise to myself that I would hide my poems, in fact, everything that I wrote, under lock and key. I had many years of productive and solitary writing, combined with lots of reading.

In 1970 I took a course on Chilean poetry that allowed me to expand my knowledge of the poetry of my country, and also to sharpen my interest in poetry and to devote more time to reading the work of my compatriots. Our profesor of Chilean Literature, Guillermo Quiñónez Ornella. was a friend of Pablo Neruda, Jorge Teillier, and of many other poets. In addition, his father, also a poet, had been a close friend of Pablo de Rokha. These stories filled my head. He tried to bring Jorge Teillier to our university but he never managed to get him to come. At this point of my life at the age of 19, I still had not had the opportunity to meet a poet. The following year, 1971, something occurred that would further motivate this timid and anonymous poet. For more than a decade in my university we had a major known as Teacher of Basic Education in Spanish, but it was only in 1969, the same year that I entered the university that a new major known as Teacher of Spanish had just been established. So we were the first students to be part of this new degree and our professors felt the need to do something to give visibility to our program. That is when Professor Quiñónez, decided to organize a large event, that soon would have a name and a program: "The Nerudian Symposia." These symposia were organized by the Department of Spanish and brought several poets and scholars of poetry to Temuco. Among them were Pablo Neruda and Juvencio Valle, both poets from the area, as well as colleagues and friends from their years in the Liceo de Hombres de Temuco, the school that Neruda and Valle both attended.

There were days, perhaps even an entire week, of activities in which there were talks and poetry recitals and at least one important individual recital by the poet who was honored at the particular symposium. Ornate leaflets and booklets of their poetry were distributed to everyone on campus and in the bookstores of Temuco. The symposia were held throughout the community. Neruda visited those places of his childhood and teenage years, which he so fondly recalled in this poetry. Many of my classmates accompanied him on these trips and certainly helped to organize them. I didn't go on these trips because my shyness and lack of confidence would not let me.

I didn't go to Carahue nor to Nueva Imperial nor to any of the places that Neruda visited nor did I appear in any of the many photographs that everyone took with him. My shyness and the resulting anonymity wouldn't allow me to make myself known. However, I attended each one of the talks and recitals that were scheduled during the symposia. I especially remember Neruda's individual recital in the largest classroom of that very young university campus. Neruda sat down, placed a few books on top of the table and read several poems according to the list of poems that he had previously prepared and then he asked the audience if there were any poems that they wished to hear him recite. Someone said "I would like you to recite "Where could Guillermina be?" and he immediately read that poem that evoked the lovely tenderness of adolescent love. Once he finished his reading, the same person asked him, "Could you tell us who Guillermina was ?" and "What was your relationship with her?" And the poet, mature and well-versed in that type of question responded that he didn't think it was prudent to talk about it since that little girl in all likelihood would be a beloved grandmother to her grandchildren and to her family in some part of Temuco and that there was no reason to reveal her name nor anything else about her.

That would be the last time that I would see Pablo Neruda in person. The first time was in Castro in my island of Chiloé when I was little boy wearing shorts and for the first time entered the theater in my town when I saw him from a distance in the gallery, applauded by a crowd in which I didn't recognize a single face. Now at no more than 4 or 5 meters away (13 or 16 feet), in broad daylight, in the second or third row of a classroom, surrounded by my classmates, my professors, and the general public in front of me, like a sun illuminating the poetry symposium. But I didn't move from my seat nor did I approach him when the recital ended, nor did I shake his hand nor congratulate him nor ask him anything because I didn't have a question nor any words in my head. I simply listened to him, listened to him, and then I went back to my room without approaching Neruda. The sun had illuminated the Temucan evening and me, a shy young man from the rainy south of Chile, knew very well how much the sun could burn. So, I didn't dare approach him.

And Neruda kept growing for everyone.

A few months later our poet was in Paris where he was informed that he had been awarded the Nobel Prize in Literature. His readers received the news in Temuco, Chiloé, Punta Arenas, Santiago, Valparaíso, Antofagasta, and everywhere on the planet where they knew his name and poetry. He received the Nobel Prize and the image of Neruda continued to grow and increase considerably at the same time that the cancer silently continued to consume him. At the beginning of September Neruda proposed to President Allende "that the State publish an edition of a million copies of an *Antología Popular* of his poetry. Neruda announced that the publishing house Losada (owner of the copyright) and the poet would not charge for the book provided that the edition be given away entirely to school students, unions and, the members of the armed forces" (Teitelboim, 378). The anthology appeared on November 20, 1972 with a preface written by President Allende and prepared in France by Neruda and his friend and secretary Homero Arce, during the month of September. This publication would be a momentous event in advance of the celebration of the Nobel Prize that would be held in the National Stadium in Santiago at the beginning of December.

Nevertheless, not everything was going well. The return of Neruda for the celebration of the Nobel Prize and to receive the love of the Chilean people would not be able to count on the presence of President Allende who was traveling outside of the country. And added to this difficulty – Neruda had already been informed about Allende's absence ahead of time – were the serious concerns about his health and the health of his country as Neruda mentioned in a letter written to his friend, Volodia Teitelboim, on October 18, 1972:

> *In addition to the worries that exist in Chilean society and the copper embargo, I have to give you another piece of bad news. The same illness has come back again and this time it's even stronger. I am once again subjected to many days of probes, injections, and antibiotics. According to the doctor, they are going to have to do what they call a cleansing, which, in reality, is an operation under general anesthesia. (379)* [1]

That unspecified disease in the letter, done so that the news would not become public, would transform the celebratory trip into a permanent stay in Chile because a few months later Neruda resigned from his diplomatic post in France.

The rest is well known. On September 11, 1973, the coup d'état occurred and 12 days later, on September 23, the poet died. Neruda's death became a tragic metaphor for the situation in the country, since the death of Neruda appears to decisively mark the end of democratic rule of Allende and of democracy in Chile in general. The President of the Republic, the nation's poet, and civic life, everything in a flash, the country felt it and suffered those loses with grief.

Nevertheless, the physical death of the poet did not mean that his spirit did not live on throughout Chile, decade after decade and publication after publication his image became engrained in the fabric of the country and, ultimately, he had become the most important icon of his country. Since the beginning of the dictatorship, Neruda's poetry (or at least much of it) was banned, and his homes were looted and destroyed. But along with the official campaign to eradicate his poetry and his image as a fighter and a free man, the Chilean people, in a completely natural process, not only took it upon themselves to preserve the image of his poetry but also to reaffirm and honor his work. His books were banned and removed from the libraries and bookstores but his poetry traveled from person to person. His name was defamed but his name, his poetry and his figure spread in a magnificent blossoming on murals, T-shirts, postcards made by artisans. Neruda, the nation's poet, became the engine of the political battle, of hope and of the battles of the people to reclaim their freedom. His poems contained messages that the young people memorized. During the 17 years of dictatorship, his image and his work became more

---

[1] Teitelboim, Volodia. Neruda. Madrid: Ediciones Michay, 1984.

polarized.

It is not easy to verify how much or how little Neruda was read during those years, but undoubtedly one can say that what was most often read of Neruda's work were those poems written on the walls, on the postcards, and in underground publications. And perhaps, for that very reason, what was most read during those years were excerpts of the Canto general, although closely followed by his timeless poems in *Twenty Love Poems* and a *Song of Despair* and his magnificent *Residence on Earth*.

In 1974 I returned to my hometown in search of security. In 1975 we began a literary workshop in Castro on the island of Chiloé, the first workshop in all of Chile, founded during the dictatorship. Many names were proposed for the workshop. Among them I remember that someone suggested "In the Shadow of Neruda". But after a brief discussion the name was tossed out because in spite of the admiration for him, these fledgling poets didn't want to be in his shadow nor that of anyone else. Those young men who began to write poetry in that group soon felt the oppression and the persecution of the dictatorship, and a few years later, now in the workforce, they would feel it again but this time even more profoundly, since they were fired from the jobs during November and December 1984.

I came to the United States in July 1989, after a coalition of opposition forces won the plebiscite and defeated Pinochet. My wife's scholarship and mine were barely enough to maintain my family. I had been in the United States for two and half years without any possibility of returning to my country, at least for a few years. So that is when Neruda appeared in my life once again. In September 1991, the Neruda Foundation informed me that I had won the Pablo Neruda Prize that year and that I should travel to Santiago in order to receive the prize. At that very moment, the poet was not just a poet but he was transformed into an object of my saintly devotion.

In 2004, the 100-year anniversary of the birth of Pablo Neruda, I invited Iván Carrasco Muñoz, the director of my thesis in Temuco, to my university to give a talk about Neruda. The room for the talk was completely filled and when his talk ended an older woman, of Russian origin and who had lived in the United States since the end of World War II, approached me and told me that she wanted to put me in touch with a friend of hers whose father had traveled throughout Chiloé and who had taken lots of photos. She also mentioned that for many years she had been looking for someone from Chiloé who could recognize the people in the photos. Since she didn't give me any more information about the trip, I thought that she was talking about a tourist who had spent time on the island, had fallen in love with the food and the scenery, and who wanted to send the photos to the people whom he had met there. It turned out that my first impression was incorrect. The truth is that the matter was much more complicated and the information that I had begun to compile about the photographer and his trip in the months that followed our brief conversation would keep me, and in fact, they continue to keep me busy for years as I work to trace the journey of that photographer, Milton Rogovin, to Chiloé at the recommendation of and with the help of Pablo Neruda.

Four decades after the death of Neruda, the poet is much more present than ever before. His poetry continues to be published everywhere, it continues to be studied each day, and it is translated time and time again. The talks and the tributes thrive all over the world in academic institutions, in labor organizations, and in cultural organizations such as this one. The image of the poet and of his poetry have become much more important and all encompassing for me each day, and the brilliance of Neruda never ceases to grow. Nevertheless, for more than about 20 years I have approached Neruda with more and more confidence; I feel that I can travel above his lines of poetry like being above a great valley or above enormous mountains of great heights and depths. Sometimes I get lost in this vast universe, but I'm not afraid of it. On the contrary, I feel completely at ease. Maybe it's because I am no longer that young boy who found himself unexpectedly seeing the poet in the Cine Rex in Castro, or perhaps the years since that chance encounter have helped to erase some of the shyness, so that I could become even closer to Neruda.

Havertown, March 2012
(The text was translated to English by Dr. Lee Abraham)

Carlos Trujillo is a Chilean poet and academic born in Castro, island of Chiloe (Chile). He is currently a professor of Hispanic American Literature at Villanova University, where he served as the Director of the Graduate Program in Hispanic Studies in addition to teaching courses on Latin American poetry and narrative. He is also leading a poetry workshop he founded 19 years ago.

In his native country he also founded and directed *Taller Literario Aumen (Aumen Literary Workshop)*, first and one the most important literary workshops in Chile during the dark years of Augusto Pinochet's dictatorship.

His books include: *Postales de Filadelfia/Postcards of Philadelphia* (English translation by Joseph Robertson), Casavaria, 2012; *Música en la pared*, Santiago: Cuarto Propio, 2010; *Texto sobre texto,* Colección Casa de Poesía, Editorial Universidad de Costa Rica, 2009; *Nada queda atrás,* Santiago: Isla Grande-MAM Chiloé, 2007; *Palabras*, Lima: Alberto Chiri Editor, 2005; *Aumen: Antología Poética*, Valdivia: Aumen, 2001; *Todo es prólogo*, New Jersey: Ediciones Nuevo Espacio, 2000; *No se engañe nadie, no. Antología de sonetos y otros poemas de Lope sin Pega*. Santiago: Mosquito Editores, 1999; *La hoja de papel,* Santiago, Chile: Aumen, 1992; *Mis límites (Antología personal 1974-1983)*, Santiago: Aumen, 1992; *Los que no vemos debajo del agua*, Santiago: Cambio, 1986; *Los territorios,* Ancud: Aumen/Cóndor, 1982; *Escrito sobre un balancín,* Ancud: Aumen/Fundechi, 1979; and *Las musas desvaídas*, Quillota: El Observador, 1977.

At present he is in the process of polishing the manuscript of his edition of the journal of the American photographer Milton Rogovin, written in Chile in 1967, and his correspondence with Pablo Neruda and some other important Chilean artists.

In 1991 Dr. Carlos Trujillo won the *Pablo Neruda Prize,* awarded by the Fundación Pablo Neruda, in Santiago, Chile.

Neruda's Irreverent Elegies

Greg Dawes

North Carolina State University

Of the many works Neruda wrote—his odes, sonnets, his avant-gardist free verse, his openly political verse, and so on—I have chosen to talk about *Elegy*, a posthumous chapbook, because it is the topic of the last chapter of the monograph I am completing on his poetry and politics from 1956 to 1973.[1] But I have also elected to talk about this work because it marks the end of Neruda's political and aesthetic evolution after the major crisis he confronted in 1956 due to Khrushchev's revelations of the crimes committed during the Stalin years. Apparently unaware of the crimes in spite of certain comments Ilya Ehrenburg had made to him on occasion, Neruda was driven into a crisis that he put on display in *Estravagario*, published in 1958. Full of irony, playful imagery and wordings, humor, self-criticism, and serious observations about his health, on the surface it appears to be, as René de Costa has noted, "very individualist, even frivolous in its self-indulgence" and an embrace of anti-poetry. [2] Yet, as I have argued, *Estravagario* is an attempt to work through the political and personal crisis that Neruda was facing at that time primarily via the form. The rebellion in form, which marks a clear break with his committed poetry—seen most clearly in *General Song* (1950)—constitutes a way to deal with the crisis, a way to internalize it. In the long run, this traumatic impasse led him to reformulate his political engagement while remaining a communist, seen in *Song of Protest* (1960) and to place the personal above the political in *One Hundred Love Sonnets* (1959). From a book dedicated to praising the Cuban revolution but not uncritically, Neruda begins moving towards an advocacy for the peaceful road to democratic socialism, which culminates in *Incitement to Nixoncide and Praise for the Chilean Revolution* (1973).

---

[1] Pablo Neruda, *Geografía infrutuosa/Incitación al nixoncidio/2000/El corazón amarrillo/Elegía* (Buenos Aires: Debolsillo, 2004).

[2] René de Costa, *The Poetry of Pablo Neruda* (Cambridge, MA: Harvard University Press, 1979): 175, 178.

Written between 1971 and 1973 and inspired by his visit to the Soviet Union with his wife Matilde Urrutia shortly after receiving the Nobel Prize, the book that concerns us here, *Elegy*, as the title itself indicates, bids farewell to comrades, living and dead, whom the poet associates with Moscow. In that regard, it is as much an elegy to the Russian capital as it is an act of mourning and praise for his dear friends who personified it. Consequently, it is very much in keeping with the definition *A Dictionary of Literary Terms* gives for elegies. Since the 16th century an elegy, according to the definition, "has come to mean a poem of mourning for an individual or a lament…for some tragic event." It can be a "serious meditative poem" or a "lament for specific people." [3]

Yet, as the renowned Neruda critic Hernán Loyola has noted, the poems in *Elegy* bear the stamp of "dramatic ambiguity" because the Chilean versemaker is bidding farewell to his dear comrades and, in responding to the tragic news of his own cancer and impending death, to himself. [4] Compounding this wavering commitment on a personal level, is the profound attachment and disengagement from what Moscow, as synecdoche of the USSR, symbolized politically. This "ambivalent commitment," if I can put it that way, is present in the very act of editing the title of this book. Significantly, Neruda excised the original reference to the Russian capital (*Elegy of Moscow*) and opted instead for *Elegy*, thus showing that the book was primarily meant to commemorate the lives of his close friends while maintaining a certain distance from the USSR's achievements and tragedies.[5] As expected, however, the unifying theme in this complex book of poetry, despite the ambiguities, deals with a deep sense of loss on both the individual and political levels. And that explains the choice of the elegiac form.

In the elegies dedicated to his then current and fallen comrades, including Soviets and exiles who sought asylum in the USSR (like Nazim Hikmet), Neruda underlines their iconoclastic characters and, in so doing, allies himself with their independent aesthetic and political commitment. His good friend Ilya Ehrenburg, the prominent Soviet novelist, journalist and translator who died in 1967, for instance, is portrayed as an "uncomfort-

---

[3] *A Dictionary of Literary Terms* (New York: Penguin, 1984), 214.
[4] See Hernán Loyola's notes on *Elegy* at the end of the book (191).
[5] Volodia Teitelboim, *Voy a vivirme: variaciones y complementos nerudianos* (Santiago/Caracas: Dolmen Editores, 1998), 164.

able friend" and a "big brother":

> Now, as I
> take steps once again on my sand,
> Ilya Grigorievich, the wrinkled,
> bristled Ehrenburg, has come by to see me
> to poke fun at my life a bit
> and give me light in his own way,
> between disillusionments, severity,
> firmness, discouragements, courage,
> and more, so much more, his generous
> dacha, his inexorable heart
> like an old sword
> on whose hilt he engraved
> a French rose
> like a sacrilegious and secret love.
> Oh, uncomfortable friend,
> oh, older brother, I am walking on
> without your harsh tenderness,
> without your wisdom's lesson. [6]

A figure who was always oscillating between allegiance and heresy even during the Stalin years, the author of *The Thaw* (1954) is described in like fashion. At the same time that he poked fun at Neruda he enlightened the Chilean, but, paradoxically, via disillusionments, severity, firmness, discouragements and valor. As Neruda comments in his memoirs, Ehrenburg provoked disillusionment particularly with regards to politics during the Stalin years. [7] Moreover, as the Chilean wordsmith indicates here, due to his long exile in Paris, his "uncomfortable friend" looked upon France like a clandestine lover. This is hardly a description of the prototypical Party militant who embraces Soviet socialism. It speaks, rather, to Ehrenburg's and Neruda's freethinking, and self-critical and critical outlook on things. Yet, Ehrenburg stayed in the USSR and dedicated himself to socialism despite or because of his defiant stances. And, consequently, Neruda longs for his "harsh tenderness" as he walks the beaches in Chile. Poems like this one and others dedicated to the Spanish architect Luis Lacasa, the Spanish sculptor Alberto Sánchez, Neruda's Russian transla-

---

[6] All translations from the Spanish are mine (152-153).
[7] Pablo Neruda, *Confieso que he vivido, undécima edición* (Buenos Aires: Editorial Losada, [1974] 1992), 282-283.

tor Savich Ovadi and the Soviet poet Seymon Kirsanov follow the traditional elegiac form, lamenting their passing and yet, in Yeats-like fashion as Helen Vendler has shown, praising and valuing the comrades in arms and letters. [8]

However, Neruda writes other elegies that stretch the definition, such as those that pay homage to comrades who are still alive. In doing so, Neruda seems to be playing with elegiac verse and thus putting into practice his own aesthetic independence while lauding the iconoclastic spirit of those being held up as examples. Thus, for instance, there are poems highlighting Lily Brik (Mayakovski's lover and Elsa Triolet's sister), Yevgeny Yevtushenko, and Bella Akmadulina (the acclaimed Russian poet and Yevtushenko's former wife). In the case of Yevtushenko there is a special affinity and different kind of brotherhood than the one Neruda shared with Ehrenburg:

> Yevtushenko is crazy,
> he is a clown,
> so they say with muted mouths.
> Come, Yevtushenko,
> let us not converse,
> we have already talked about everything
> before arriving here on this world,
> and there is in your verse
> rays of a new moon,
> electronic petals,
> train engines,
> tears,
> and from time to time, hello!
> up! down!
> your pirouettes, your acrobatics on high.
> And why not be a clown?
>
> Our world is left wanting them
> Napoleon, a clown on the battlefields
> (lost later in the snow)
> Picasso, a clown of the cosmos,

---

[8] Helen Vendler, "Matter on Various Length Scales: Poetry," *Proceedings of the American Philosophical Society*, Vol. 145, No. 4 (December 2001): 395.

> dancing on the altar
> of miracles,
> and Columbus, that sad clown
> humbled by his errant ways
> discovered us centuries ago.
>
> They only won't leave the poet alone,
> they want to seize his pirouette,
> they want to rob him of his mortal leap.

Up to this point in the poem Neruda focuses on capturing Yevtushenko's jovial and clownish character, which challenges literary conventions and opens up creative possibilities. To prove that point, Neruda uses his own humorous remarks ("so they said with their mouths muted" and "let us not converse") to echo the playfulness of Yevtushenko's own work (hello! up! down!). But being a clown is, following Greek tragedy, also its mirror opposite. Napoleon was a clown in military history who lost his decisive battle in Russia in 1812 owing in part to his own blunders. Picasso, as Neruda points out, was also a jester willing to break any taboos (including dancing on altars of canonical art), and Columbus too, the discoverer of the Americas, because of his errant voyages is described as a clown. But being a prangster, a wit or a jester is off limits for poets, according to Neruda, because they are beholden to serious mediations on mortality and immortality, without being granted their own "mortal leap." In the Soviet context, quite clearly, this is a reference to the strict limitations of pre-programmed socialist realism, which Neruda denounces here indirectly and directly in his book *Isla Negra* (*Memorial de Isla Negra*).

So what follows is Neruda's defense of Yevtushenko and his joining the rebellious author of *The Heirs of Stalin* (1961) as a jester on the stage:

> I defend him
> against the new philistines.
> Onward Yevtushenko,
> let us show our skills and our sorrow,
> our pleasure at playing with light
> in the circus
> so that truth flashes
> between shadows and shadows.
> Hurrah!
> now let us take the stage,

> lights out and let the reflectors
> illuminate our faces
> so they can see
> two elated birds
> ready to cry for everybody. (162-163)

Joined grammatically the two poets then enact a tragedy with "sorrow" and the "pleasure of playing with the light," the consequence of which is to shed light on the shadows of life. Portrayed as archetypal clowns, the poets are illuminated by the stage on which they find themselves and provide illumination as they too, dialectically, join in the suffering. Here, then, as in the case of other Soviet writers and exiles in the USSR, Neruda holds up the example of a poet who became a spokesperson for post-Stalin period generation, was influenced by Mayakovsky—another iconoclast venerated by Neruda—denounced anti-semitism in the USSR, became an momentary outcast by publishing his *A Precocious Autobiography* in English, and yet was and remained a communist. In providing portraits of comrades like Yevtushenko, Neruda means to ally himself unmistakably with the Russian poet and, simultaneously, to express his lament by writing this elegy. Aware of his own impending death and mindful that he might not see Yevtushenko again, this type of elegy bids farewell not with solemnity but with humor (as the Russian would have liked it).

Significantly, Neruda begins *Elegy* with depictions of his dear companions and then proceeds to the elegies of Moscow per se, thereby representing the urbanscape as a reflection of human intervention, and providing a contrast between these favorable portraits and some of the unsavory episodes in Russian and Soviet history. Poem "V" launches the section on the Russian capital:

> Moscow, city with immense wings,
> albatross on the steppe,
> the brittle Kremlin as its nest
> and Saint Basil and its toyshop,
> city that also has a rectangular soul,
> with neighborhoods that are infinitely grey,
> cubes just out of the factories
> and the river
> meandering like a fortified arm
> 'round the fortress' waist.

Depicted as an albatross and a fortress defended by the Moskva River in this first stanza, Moscow is, nonetheless, conceived as a personified city. Though the capital's architecture and layout are lauded, it takes on a human form—with the references to its "rectangular soul" and its "fortified arm"—and thus dovetails with the portrayals of his comrades at the beginning of the book. In the long stanza that follows, that personification continues along with references to those who defended the city and made its survival possible.

> Silent and powerful city,
> maybe in old age a Gothic star,
> maybe in the recondite domain
> of seashell-shaped cathedrals
> of midway points brought down
> until they bent over the hard stature
> of Czar Ivan and Stalin the terrible,
> center of time sometimes submerged
> and other times zeniths
> which can be discerned throughout the land:
> ancient stones, vertical saints,
> dark temples like prisons,
> cupolas with golden nipples,
> white dance halls where
> decorated names that fell
> float like red carnations in the war:
> and a ardent and silent energy
> like a bonfire under the sea. (154-155)

Neruda offers a contrast between the symbolically high points of the capital, seen as zeniths in history of the capital and the nation, and the low points in which the city becomes "submerged," particularly so under the equated tyranny of "Czar Ivan and Stalin the terrible." In a series of visually inspired frames, the eloquence of the city's architecture, which marks its tremendous accomplishments, is thus juxtaposed with the history of political repression. Yet the "decorated names that fell like red carnations" in World War II, managed to preserve Moscow's radiant beauty despite being submerged by history's tragedies. In this and other poems the city becomes emblematic of, as Neruda puts it in poem VII, "the human tide" (155), while simultaneously being the locus of political terror.

What one senses here is that Moscow and the hope it held for humanity are both celebrated and perceived as a partial loss. In poem XXIV, for example, the poet as witness reimagines the moment in which the Russian revolution took place, with Lenin at its helm, yet Neruda underscores that that historical event was, in fact, an experiment. A "difficult and naked October," he says, "took on an unknown truth" (170). In other words, as Lenin's own correspondence indicated after the revolution, the future was uncertain. The Bolshevik revolution was the social revolt that wasn't supposed to happen. In a leap of history it had bypassed the European revolutions that would take place in the coming years and would prove to be unsustainable. That is why the Chilean bard considers Moscow, and thus Russia, "the fragile constructor of greatness" (170). To be sure, it offers another elegy but it is somewhat measured in its praise.

In large part, Neruda's punctuated reserve with regards to the USSR, though accompanied my certain hope, is due to the purges during the Stalin years. As he does in the best known yet largely ignored section of his book *Isla Negra* (*Memorial de Isla Negra*)—"The Episode"—Neruda carries out a caustic critique of Stalin and the Stalinist period. In *Elegy* he considers that God and the Devil "installed themselves in [Stalin's] soul." While Stalin was a "clear captain of his people" during World World II, according to the poet, the land "filled with his punishments, / every garden had its hangman" (171). In poems XXIX and XXX his criticism mounts to such a degree that one could rightly describe them as anti-elegies that tarnish the positive image the poet projects of Moscow. The capital's very identity, its history, to borrow Marx's famous phrase in *The 18th Brumaire of Louis Bonaparte,* "weighs like a nightmare on the brains of the living" due to the Stalin years. The personal and political crisis that ensued in 1956 remains, and the terrible sense of loss and guilt still haunt Neruda.

In addition to the elegies for his comrades and to a personified Moscow, we find those dedicated to death in general, foreshadowing his own. Indeed, Hernán Loyola and Volodia Teitelboim see these poems, and the book as a whole, as elegies to himself in the final analysis. [9] Afflicted with cancer for the last years of his life, it is in Moscow that he receives the confirmation that his case is terminal. After trying to digest this news, Neruda and Matilde headed back to France, where he held the post as Chilean ambassador, and then back to Chile definitively. These meditations and lamentations were written, presumably, over the span of two years.

See Hernán Loyola's notes to the book (191) and Volodia Teitelboim's *Voy a vivirme,* 486.

In poem XII Neruda imagines death as turning one into a statue, like the statues of Pushkin, Mayakovsky and Gogol in the USSR. These monuments, he remarks,

> are bitter
> because time remains
> deposited in them, rusted,
> and though flowers eventually cover
> their cold feet, the flowers are not kisses,
> they also arrive only to perish (160).

Statues, like death, he concludes in his reflections on the one erected to Mayakovsky, are

> marble, bronze or stone of a wounded animal who left
> and abandoned this congealed vestige,
> a gesture, an immobile movement,
> a casting-off of the soul (161).

Like the streets, the city's bustle and its architecture, the statues offer a likeness, the vestiges of human contact and creation, but cannot hope to rescue the friends for whom he writes elegies nor the Russian writers to whom these statues were erected. Nor can it save him personally from death, from his own movement being immobilized.

Poem XVIII elaborates on this deep lament for the loss of his comrades:

> I know, I know, neither walls, nor machines, nor bakeries
> were made by the dead:
> maybe it is so, without a doubt, but
> buildings do not nourish my soul,
> factories do not improve my health,
> nor sadness.
>
> My grief is for those
> who roamed me, who gave me sunlight,
> who communicated existences to me,
> and now what should I do with the
> soldiers' and engineers' heroism?
> Where's the grin

> or the communicative painting,
> or the teaching word,
> or the laughter, of laughter,
> the clear outburst of laughter
> of those I lost along those streets,
> around this time, around these parts
> where did I remain and they
> continue, until they finished their voyage? (166)

The negations associated with the absence of the dead, who do not erect walls, make machines or bakeries, are subsequently negated in the second half of the first stanza by the poem's speaker. Here the results of one's labor prove to be insufficient just like, we could infer, the poet's verse, because it doesn't lead to the substance of human relations, to life shared among friends. His grief and profound sense of loss goes beyond the statue, beyond the fruits of labor, to the ephemeral acts shared in comradeship: the "communicative painting," the "teaching word," the "laughter" and the "outburst of laughter." And of those who were engineers and heroic soldiers, but also of those who "gave [him] sunlight," "communicated existences" and who "roamed [him]." They continued on their way to their destination, he concludes, whereas he remained. In an indirect way Neruda is also commenting on the limitations of elegies, mere statues after all, and he is addressing the demarcations of poetry and of life itself. No matter what he does, death keeps on encroaching on his life.

Neruda returns to this topic in poem XXI:

> Because it is one thing if engraved names,
> shine or are extinguished,
> in a book or on a gravestone.
> It is not that, no, it is not about that,
> about unhusked immortality,
> it is about personal people,
> with whom one loved or ate,
> each of them unique, folded
> into his silence or his intensity.
>
> And I will not miss or unmiss,

Zygmunt Bauman, *Mortality, Immortality and Other Life Strategies* (Stanford: Stanford University Press, 1992), 55-58.

> no to importance, yes to circumstance,
> the should and have is others' worry,
> of the cruelly opinionated,
> I want for them what was nothing,
> to come back to the home in which you breathe
> and it is not just man and wife
> but rather that air, and to breathe a word
> to communicate about the impossible. (168)

Neruda seems less concerned here with, in Zygmunt Bauman's words, his or his friends' "durable significance" and his and their place in history, and more interested in underlining and eulogizing the ephemeral lived and common experiences. [10] As he notes in the second stanza, he values the fleeting but invaluable shared "circumstance" over the "importance," what appears to be "nothing" but is the essence of human relations: the shared living in the face of our own indecipherable existence. An impossible, indecipherable life then leads to a meditation on death, in short, a classical and profound lament about life's passing.

Though I haven't been able to do it justice here, *Elegy* is one of Neruda's most well-crafted and moving books of poetry, which addresses his sorrow yet praise for those who joined him in his life experiences and which reflects his own attempts to come to terms with his impending death. At the same time, it is a farewell to those comrades, but also to the Soviet Union. On the one hand, it is a leave-taking in a literal sense of the Soviet geographic space, history and people tied to Neruda's own mortality. On the other hand, it marks an important confirmation of the poet's evolution dialectically beyond Soviet socialism (without negating it). We get a sense of that in the last poem, which closes with reflections on capitalism and the future of humanity (socialism):

> you and I, who live on the limits
> of the old world and of the new worlds
> participate with melancholy
> in the fusion of the two contrary winds,
> in the unity of the times that march on.
> Life is space in movement(174).

It would be easy to conclude that Neruda is advocating for social democracy here, but it is worth keeping in mind that he was writing this during the Popular Unity's and Allende's socialist experiment in Chile. Like

Incitement to Nixoncide and Praise for the Chilean Revolution, then, *Elegy* pays homage to the socialist path in Chile while recognizing and yet limiting the Soviet Union's role as the originator of modern socialism and as a nostalgic source of inspiration.

Greg Dawes is professor of Latin American Studies and Cultural Theory at North Carolina State University and editor of the peer reviewed electronic journal, *A Contracorriente*. Greg Dawes is from the United States, but spent seven years of his childhood in Argentina and has spent time in several other Latin American countries as well, particularly Chile. His books include *Aesthetics and Revolution: Nicaraguan Poetry, 1979-1990, Verses Against the Darkness: Pablo Neruda's Poetry and Politics*, and *Poetas Ante La Modernidad: Las Ideas Esteticas y Politicas de Vallejo, Huidobro, Neruda y Paz*. He is currently working on *La luz prismática y la oscuridad determinante: Pablo Neruda después de 1956*.

☙

*Fourth Annual
Nâzım Hikmet
Poetry Competition*

Poetry Competition Selection Committee
(*in alphabetical order*)

Greg Dawes
See Page 35

Joseph Donahue
Joseph Donahue is a poet and the author of *Before Creation*, *Monitions of the Approach*, *WorldWell Broken*, *Incidental Eclipse*, *Terra Lucida* and most recently *Dissolves*. Along with Leonard Schwartz and Edward Foster, he edited the anthology of contemporary poetry, *Primary Trouble*. With Edward Foster he edited a volume of essays, *The World in Space and Time, Towards a History of Innovative American Poetry 1970-2000*. He is a *Professor of the Practice* in the English department at Duke University.

Dorianne Laux
Dorianne Laux's most recent collections are *The Book of Men* and *Facts about the Moon*. A finalist for the National Book Critics Circle Award, and winner of the Oregon Book Award, Laux is also author of *Awake*, *What We Carry*, and *Smoke* from BOA Editions, as well as a fine press edition, *Dark Charms*, from Red Dragonfly Press. She teaches poetry in the MFA Program at North Carolina State University and is founding faculty at Pacific University's Low Residency MFA Program.

Murat Nemet-Nejat
Poet, translator and essayist, he edited and largely translated *Eda: An Anthology of Contemporary Turkish Poetry* (2004), translated *Orhan Veli, I*, Orhan Veli (1989), Ece Ayhan, *A Blind Cat Black and Orthodoxies* (1997), and Seyhan Erözçelik, *Rosestrikes and Coffee Grinds* (2010). He is the author of *The Peripheral Space of Photography* (2004) and, recently, the memoir/essay *Istanbul Noir* (2011), the poems *steps* (2008), *Prelude* (2009), *Disappearances* (2010) and *Alphabet Dialogue/Penis Monologues* (2010). His poem *The Structure of Escape* will be published by Talisman House in 2011. He is presently working on the long poem *The Structure of Escape*.

Tanya Olson

Tanya Olson lives in Durham, North Carolina and teaches at Vance-Granville Community College. Her work has been published in *Boston Review*, *Beloit Poetry Review*, *Cairn*, *Fanzine*, *Bad Subjects*, *Main Street Rag*, *Pedestal Magazine*, *Elysian Fields*, and *Southern Cultures*. In 2010, she won a *Discovery / Boston Review* prize and was named a 2011 Lambda Fellow by the Lambda Literary Foundation.

Hatice Örün Öztürk

Hatice Örün Öztürk is a Teaching Associate Professor in Electrical and Computer and Biomedical Engineering departments at North Carolina State University. Throughout her career, she pursued mathematics and languages together. Her poems were published by different magazines in Turkey. Her translations of *Mahmoud Darwish* poems from Arabic to Turkish were published by *Varlık*. She is working on her first book of poems *Ekmek ve Takvim* (*Bread and Calendar*) which will be published by *Pan* in Istanbul, Turkey.

Finalists

(In alphabetical order)

Hala Alyan

Palestinian-American

Dowry:
eyelid canvas of seaside village
snaked with electricity and rooftops.

Fraud:
I love the jaws of another city.

Daughter:
of refugees?
Mourn the silhouette-

self, the hennaed version.
Arable girl.

Love:
luck-wedding, soil
of cobwebs. Mine.

Gaza:
starflowers my mouth,
only teeth-poems. Only pomegranate seeds.

Misplace:
enormously. Brother
and sister,

gift is spine-
fury. I call to myself as minarets do.

Hala Alyan

Maktoub*

She boils water, the
steam marbling her veil, fine-

misting her brow. The curfew
has lifted and the children

are coming for dinner. The children's
children, too. This seizes

her throat like a joy, the
clamor that is about to rattle

the small house. She dips the grape
leaves, one by one, into the water, petite-

skirted as miniature kimonos. In
water, their dull skin shines. Next,

the rice tumbles in. She wants to talk to
Aida, prettiest granddaughter, nearly

seventeen, about what the
butcher's uncle had confided:

they saw Aida at the beach
in a skimpy yellow bikini, lotus-

flowering with her hands as
music played and a man with the

Hala Alyan

haircut of a soldier clapped. Rolling
the grape leaves is her favorite part,

it seems illicit. As a teenager, she smoked
hashish once, and giggled for hours. Flat

against the cutting board, the leaves seem akin
to starfish or shamrocks. Wet, their green

is gorgeous. It is impossible,
raising girls in war. The rice is ready.

When she drains it, the fluid runs
colorless. They will break

or be broken, dance
for enemy men or wilt like

flags. She torsos the leaves with
rice, rolls them tightly. Stanchly,

they fold for her. The
smartest girls are catlike, plucking

scraps, turning bullets into
pendants, using glass to frame

pictures. She sets the table, lights the taupe
candle, her favorite. Under the flame's dome,

Hala Alyan

the meal glistens emerald. (The smartest
find something to polish.) She

wants to tell Aida to put her hands
to better use, to pound love

out of cloves, pinch the mouths
of wooden pins open and nestle in

clothes for the sun to dry. She wants
to say hope can be the cruelest

mother of all. Better to tell yourself April
was built for battle. May, burial.

*Arabic for 'It is written'

Hala Alyan

Sahar & her Sisters

i.

Ink-haired quartet, born summers apart, they left
their mother gasping, mouth dry. Womb limp
as a starfish. Their father set fire to the midwife after the

fourth, rammed into his wife bark etched with holy verses
to free her of the cancer that is girl. This is what is meant by setting.
Sahar and her sisters move like snakes through the seasons, cinder-

eyed, dizzy-hearted. They dig lungs in the soil. Elongated bones,
lunching on goat meat, they grow with the chaos of carnivores.
This is what is meant by lullaby. Sahar and her sisters call each

other Magda, short for Magdalene, short for the disaster of fetus.
They apprentice within gynic hallways. Uterus as asylum to the
things they learn to erase. What does not wither will grow and

Sahar and her sisters build a hut at the river's edge, charge
camel bones for their magic. The women arrive. Feather-spined,
earth-damned and tired, they come to be emptied. This is what

is meant by mercy. Clusters, token of semen and humidity, dahlia-
tinted, they are a luxury of red. A froth. Sahar and her sisters train
their own ovaries like a militia. Menstruate with the precision of

choir practice. This is what is meant by romance. When a story comes
to the village about women who love women, women who drain
women, the fathers say, *Close your legs, daughters*. Say,
You don't love the way that I love so that can't be love.

Hala Alyan

ii.

It is foxes,
foxes that come
sniffing

the
river's edge, foxes
that find

Sahar and her sisters,
ink-haired quartet,
hanging

like constellations
from the trees.

Hala Alyan

Hala Alyan is a Palestinian-American poet who has lived in various parts of the Middle East and the United States. Currently, she resides in Brooklyn, where she is pursuing a doctoral degree in the field of psychology. Hala has a collection of poetry, entitled *Atrium*, forthcoming by Three Rooms Press.

Peter Blair

Captain Adam on Mars

> Tribes Picked by U.S. to Fight Taliban, Get Tied Up in Own Feud;
> 'If They Take Our Land, We'll Kill Them All.'
> *Wall Street Journal,* 2011

Hot dust swirls off the hill
like an ambush, tribes on each side
each ready to kill the other over a patch
of arid scrub. The American, Adam,
sits between two turbaned chieftains
the Ali Sher Kel's and the Sepai
keeping a flimsy trust, unclear
as the patches of olive green, desert
gray, blended beneath his stripes.

He must speak to them in parables:
*He who loves his fellow man loves
democracy.* Captain Adam refuses
to give guns to either side
in this mountain landscape that's *like Mars
on a good day*. "Democrazy,"
his lieutenants joke off duty on the base.

Captain Adam opens his shirt.
They touch the bullet-proof
vest thinking it's an air-conditioner.
They finger the black steel ammo clips
lined up in pockets across his chest,
and point at his perfect white teeth.
What century is it on Mars?

Peter Blair

Portrait of My Mother in Winter

My saw slices through logs as she speaks
of the floods, smoke, and orange glowing
clouds of her childhood in the dark house
on Suisman Street. Her lawn chair sunk
in wet snow, she leans back in a white leather
jacket, a clear martini gleaming in her hand.

The saw's teeth sing through bark
and a sweet sassafras smell rises. She escaped
Pittsburgh for D.C., the 1930's, riding horses
with her friends on rolling Bethesda Hills
among clear skies and clean rivers.

The logs fall to the ground showing rings
of milky heartwood by the cabin
my father bought us years before he died.
She stares out into the late brightness
of afternoon through bare trees,
speaking not to me but to the blank dazzle
on the snow. In love with my father's
navy whites, she left college, eloped to Florida.

Sawdust coats my boots. The blade's raspy voice
asks no questions as logs pile up like money
in the bank. She saw him off to war
at Laguna Beach, then drove her mother
and his from California to Pittsburgh:
a punctured tire in Arizona, the clapboard
motels, the *God-cursed dust* of the flat
two-lane roads of Oklahoma.

Peter Blair

I hang the saw on a nail in the shed,
stack the pile of logs in a half-chord
along the cabin wall. She can't remember
why they settled back in Pittsburgh
among the mills and blast furnaces.
We could have gone anywhere, she says,
a wry smile on her lips, and sips the gin.

Peter Blair

After an Argument, We Explore Pittsburgh

In the Diamond Market, white-coated men
dump pigs' legs, turkey necks,
chicken hearts into cases. Munching faces
stare at us through sweating windows.

You wander away to the square
where pigeons peck brown grass
around a gaunt, bearded rag-picker
feeding them. All his possessions hang
in plastic bags from his crutches.

Clouds float close to the sidewalk
trapped in the huge window panels
of the Pittsburgh Plate Glass Building,
immoveable, locked in blue squares,
like a painting by Magritte.

By the Duquesne Club's sandblasted pilasters
Cadillacs line the curb in front,
while bashed-in dumpsters on wheels
park in the alley waiting to be tipped.

At Water Street, the sky opens up
and sunlight flashes off the river.
Along the wharf, high-speed ramps
crisscross in front of buildings.

Peter Blair

Walking under the roadway
between rows of cement pillars,
we breathe in a dank cave-smell.
Iron rings for tying up 10,000 ton barges
hang from the pillars that hold up the city.

Reflected light undulates
up and down their rounded lengths.
We lean against one and kiss,

your back against the scars
where the concrete's crumbled away
and rusted tie-rods show through.

This is the first place in the city to flood.
Young kids sense something wild and fated
among the hundreds of columns.

They write their names on them:
Serge, Lurk, Hick-dog, Captain Cock,
as if claiming their futures.

Peter Blair

Peter Blair's most recent book of poems is *Farang* (2010) published by Autumn House Press. His previous books include, *The Divine Salt* (2003, Autumn House Press) and *Last Heat*, which won the Washington Prize in 1999 and was published by Word Works Press. Born in Pittsburgh, he has worked in a steel mill, a psychiatric ward, and served three years in the Peace Corps. He currently lives in Charlotte, North Carolina with his wife and son.

Kevin Boyle

Reading the Bible With My Lapdog On My Lap

At any sound—the children moving upstairs, the fridge
Rumbling to a stop, the cat next door licking its paws—
My dog would almost foam at the mouth, yelling
About injustice, infringement, the terrors of night,
But when I read the Bible silently, how quiet she became
On my lap, warming my little dancing heart,
Asking, finally, how she was portrayed there
In Holy Writ. In Holy Writ it is written, I began,
That you return to your own vomit, darling,
You lounge with sorcerers and those who practice falsehoods,
You have a mighty appetite and lick even the sores
Of lepers, and you should not be given that which is holy,
Nor, likewise, should swine get tossed pearls.
She agreed with the latter, hating pigs who, once cleaned,
Returned to their mire to wallow, but the rest made her feel
Unloved, excluded, like a Cain among animals,
A pariah with a glossy coat. I said, Be not afeared,
I only read this for sport, I am not a thumper of Bibles,
I believe that when you die and I bury you among
The hollies that abut our land, you will be in a maggoty
Paradise of unknowing, your appetite contained,
Your desire for balls being thrown silenced,
And when I join you, we will be brought together
In a feast of emptiness, all of my commands now questions
The soil will answer. Oh master, she said, that is
Not paradise, but eternal gloom, my bark equal to my bite
But zero in the tally, my happy tail unwaggable.
And I: So be it, for it is so ordained, let us cry together
Now, and so we did, her eyes glisteny, fly-free,
Lambent, and she licked the sores of my open face
Imagining what we would become. Easy, girl, easy.

Kevin Boyle

The 100%

The Occupy Graveyard movement began with the death
Of the town's poor, the "women of the house"
And the long-time members of the Grace Baptist Evangelical
House of Worship and Divine Intercession, gathering up
Their scant belongings and teat-dragging dogs into
The orange clay, their chants of "Give me liberty, damn it,
Or give me death" finally answered with death.
Then the tumored rats, the birds with one good wing,
Squirrels who had fallen from high branches of willow oaks
Were laid to rest, their thought bubbles beside them
In the grass: Death to the cars and all godforsaken armaments.
Then the drunken teens on meth and OxyContin, methadone
Mixed with heroin, died in their sleep or asleep briefly
At the wheel, yelling out as they were laid to rest, Speed,
Greater Speed! Then bank tellers behind bulletproof glass
And on telescreens were placed in Plexiglas mausoleums,
Their bodies transported through town in pneumatic tubes,
Saying as they arrived, Thank you for banking us in.
Even those paying 9% taxes on their first 700,000
And 8% on the rest, with the deduction of 20 dollars
To the Inhumane Society factored in, even they perished,
Composing letters to the editor about tax relief as they decomposed.
All those masturbating were dragged by their free hand
Down Church Street, dying as they came to a stop among the mounds
And holes, I among them. Taxis became gurneys, pews long stretchers,
Parkas, jumpers and fleeces so many palls
And everyone inside their winter clothes were called pallbearers
To simplify everything. When the movement succeeded, its demands
Met in spades, the sound of rejoicing came from
The rivers, and the long rains, the gutters filled with leaves
Just overflowing their lips, that restful sound that even the insomniacs
Once found so soothing, the sound of wearing down and washing away.

Kevin Boyle

Ham Is Toast, Ham I Am

How often would my brothers have the drill
of carrying a cloak or towel between
their shoulders and walking backwards
towards my seated father, and my father would say,
Thou art like Japheth, Brian, and thou unto Shem, John,
and I would always ask, And who am I, Father?
Even at the 4th of July three-legged races,
my brothers would walk backwards, a flag
between their shoulders, my father at the finish line,
saying, when the flag arrived on his lap, God
shall enlarge Japheth and dwell in the tents of Shem.
And I, will I be enlarged or have my pup tent dwelt in?
It seemed morbid or icily clairvoyant to me
when my brothers would walk backwards
toward my father lying in his sleep, the beautiful pall
between their shoulders that they'd clumsily
place on him without looking, sometimes
covering only his thrombotic legs, sometimes
covering only his wheeze, and I would sing,
To the left, to the left, to provide aid,
but they would never harken, only cast
aspersions my way, though they did not face my face.
I asked my mother for her insights through
the bathroom door, eyeing her nakedness
in the keyhole as she rubbed spices into her skin,
and she said, My child, you are the youngest
and so must suffer as I have suffered. I thought
to slam your head against stone when you were born—
a precious babe—but then John would be the youngest.

Kevin Boyle

You are cursed, ok? I put my finger
to the hole and made her disappear, and walked
backwards away from there, in shock, the scent
of her spices even in my eyes that burnt,
even unto the pages of my diary in which I wrote,
Today was an alright day, I guess,
in that I learned, in part, the cause.

Kevin Boyle's book, *A Home for Wayward Girls*, won the New Issues Poetry Prize and was published in 2005 and his chapbook, *The Lullaby of History*, won the Mary Belle Campbell Poetry Chapbook Prize and was published in 2002. His poems have appeared in *Alaska Quarterly*, *Antioch Review*, *Colorado Review*, *Denver Quarterly*, *Greensboro Review*, *The Michigan Quarterly Review*, *Natural Bridge*, *North American Review*, *Northwest Review*, *Poet Lore*, *Poetry East*, *storySouth* and *Virginia Quarterly Review*. He was one of the finalists of the 2011 Nazim Hikmet Poetry Competition. Originally from Philadelphia, Kevin now lives in North Carolina and teaches at Elon University.

Photo by Tess Boyle

Amy Leigh Brown

Speak Devotion

we speak devotion
and it chimes
with purity ancient as church bells
assume no practice
measures
purity
as likely it is purulent
giving way like our flesh
if we merely lie upon
one spot for too long

devotion versus habit an
attending to fearlessly
loyal may be just a shade off
neurotic obsession
tending
requires
tendering
of soul stock
time needed for gathering
nest straw

Amy Leigh Brown

speak devotion
imply
unwavering supplication
a love stain shading
all action infused
a bowing down
a bowing down
a lowering to
enable the levering
extrication of the heart
from darkness through deed

speak devotion
worry the motive
specter of betrayal
take your shadow off
my quarry
i must build
my nest anew
light candles on my
unsheltered way
a light to hide from
your hungry dark

Amy Leigh Brown

A Bird's Guide to the Field

the falcon broke
tether still shuttered
to find the others
building their city
as Aristophanes scribed
after waking one
day with a feather in
his mouth inhaling
choked coughing
frowning with knowledge
owl watched from a
far pine

with the unquestioning
certainty of one
acting in trance
the hooded void
a psychomanteum
where anthems hum in fractuous
rays which speak on wavelengths
coded with the weight
the entification of all
being past and spoken
crushed into layers
an archeological barcode
a radio where all the stations
play at once
your life
and all it was
and was and
will

Amy Leigh Brown

this tower is for the falcon
that burdened cipher
who comes not to rest
but with purpose elided
crests hermaion
provoked by the allusive topography
of the vision

Amy Leigh Brown

llad dafad dall

sing a song of six pants
a pocket full of wool
wool of full pocket a
priori postulation
transcendental not
merely cognate
if falsely so
origin unknown
you haunt a valley
tethered as martyr
pall of absent vision
vision absent of pall
full they are of weeping

Amy Leigh Brown

Amy Leigh Brown grew up in rural Piedmont, North Carolina, her father's only son. Her academic training is in chemistry and molecular medicine. Her poetry is published here for the first time.

Hedy Habra

Writing in dust

Let's weave braids of dust rich
with time's unspeakable
debris, broken voices, whispers,
dried tears, insects' wings.

Doesn't most of it come from
our discarded skin?

Or is it the residue of fleeting
breaths hidden in pillow edges
and seams, my kitten's fur,
conjuring my old cat's scent
alive in this impalpable,
minute form?

And is it true you can clone someone
with just one hair, one speck of flesh,
all of which hovers around you?

Some say don't clean too much,
a house full of dust is a sign
of laughter, of good times
spent forgetting how to clean.

Some say chasing spider webs
in every nook and corner isn't healthy
while unaware of those nesting
in one's mind.

Hedy Habra

Let's shake the dust in our heart
watch it fall like snow in a crystal globe,
paint open shutters, let the wind in

or think of what we might
write in our own dust
as on a sandy shore,
express the unthinkable,

unravel what informs that dust,
let it settle at will,
heavy as sand in an hourglass.

Hedy Habra

I Always Knew I Was a Sibyl at Heart

I have paid my dues and fought mood swings
before entering that stage of well-earned wisdom
preventing me from climbing over walls in midday,
pacing labyrinthine pathways or drowning
in the deep wells of insomnia.

I've collected enough books to keep me company
till the day I die, stacked in double and triple rows,
in an arbitrary order they refute in unison. Each
volume stares at me with eyes shut, scrutinizes
my movements, tries to lure me into caressing
its spine, opening it like an I Ching.

Shouldn't I, on account of my years, be granted
the Sight, recognize the rhythm of unspoken speech
in the folds of each palm, read the veins of each leaf
blown by the wind? I could be scrying in the moonlight,
eyes wide-open like a wise owl sensing the slightest
reflection on still water.

Hedy Habra

Weaving and Unweaving

I used to marvel at my mother's readiness
                to unravel a sweater
      or unstitch

her needlepoint
        at the slightest error. Eyes fixed
                over colored wool or silk
           sliding through needles,

her racing fingers
        fiddled in silence,
erasing long working hours.

      But why look at unweaving as erasure,

           or as Penelope's endless fight against time?

Isn't it rather a way to retrace one's steps?

                Each gesture,
     an intimate journey into the weaver's
memory?

          I think of the backwards movement
of the needle,
      unstitching every design,
          yarn by yarn
                as one erases a word,
          letter by letter.

Hedy Habra

Each stitch removed leaves an imprint
            on the fabric or loom,   a gaping space
       like footsteps,

        the way the tip of a pencil
                    scars paper fibers,

its invisible indentations
       only revealed by a brush of charcoal dust.

A careful erasure revisits the pattern. The image

        vanishes, not the roads that led to it,
                like a text whose lines haunt you

as you discard them one by one.

        A constant wavering between
                remembering and forgetting,
telling and retelling.

Hedy Habra

Hedy Habra, born and raised in Egypt, is of Lebanese origin. She received her MFA and a PhD in Spanish Literature from Western Michigan University where she currently teaches. Her poetry and fiction in French, Spanish and English have appeared in numerous journals and anthologies, including *Puerto del Sol*, *The New York Quarterly*, *Cider Press Review*, *Nimrod*, *Cutthroat*, *Poet Lore*, *Inclined to Speak*, *Poetic Voices Without Borders Vol 2*, and *Dinarzad's Children Second Edition*. Her critical essays have appeared in *Latin American Literary Review*, *Chasqui and Inti*, among others. Her collection of short stories, *Flying Carpets* was published by March Street Press and her scholarly book *Mundos alternos y artísticos en Vargas Llosa* is forthcoming from *Iberoamericana/Vervuert*.

Jeffrey Kahrs

Dying Light Sonnet

It isn't. The shuttling loom
laces clouds with dusty, red thread
as a deckhand pulls on the line
and we go into the Bosphorus'
undulating ripples of light.
Like any seaman he knows
the confident, steady walk of calm water
as he clambers up the stairs
to the wheelhouse and waits
till it's time to loop the line
round the bollards. So it is with light,
ferried to and from transformers.
And darkness. Dying its strands
and spinning our days.

Jeffrey Kahrs

Lost & Foundling Sonnet

I want to see more *Jeffness*. Dear friend, I know
I've tethered my immortal soul to ancient formalities,
but it's only months since I moved. Everywhere red delicious
are dropping, but charts of our Gowanda still hang from the walls:
Some days its *sang*—song of blood tomes on a bass drum—
other times aimless hours soak the day's cloth, hanging from me
with the weight of their soft rain. Live among words
and soon you're wearing their burdens.
Pledge right now, right hand raised, it wasn't just the butler
in the library with a crowbar, but the cogent squawking
of riddle, solve and riddle again. I'll tell you this,
it's no miracle how infants pile up on the front step.
A whole world's out there doing it—I mean looking for
continents, but me, it's enough just to feed these kids.

Jeffrey Kahrs

I Know You Said

static is the inevitable
and frightening position of placing
my ear to the shell
of our conversation

knowing who we are
dismembers our words

breaks apart our timbre

makes *terra incognita* a
known fact

This is how
we sailed round every headland
to face the headwind

and still it sounds less
like rocks than the splash
in the great pond

we are exquisitely
transforming into ripples
of ourselves

Jeffrey Kahrs

Jeff Kahrs was born in the Hague, Netherlands, and raised in California. He received a B.A. in Dramatic Literature from U.C. Santa Cruz and an M.A. from Boston University, where he studied with Derek Walcott and Leslie Epstein. In 1988 Jeff helped found a reading series in Seattle called *Radio Free Leroy's*, which ran for six years. From 1993 to 2011 he lived in Istanbul, where he taught English in its myriad forms. He co-edited an issue of the *Atlanta Review* on poetry in Turkey, was published in *Subtropics*, *mediterranean.nu*, and had a chapbook e-published through *Gold Wake Press*. More recently he co-edited a section of the Turkish magazine *Çevirmenin Notu* on English-language poets in Istanbul, and he was published in *Talisman: A Journal Of Contemporary Poetry And Poetics*. Drawing on his experience as a commercial fisherman in Alaska, Jeff is currently writing a history of the Deep Sea Fishermen's Union of the Pacific to celebrate their 100th anniversary.

Daniel Abdal-Hayy Moore

The Predicament

The predicament is there is no predicament
everything turns into a butterfly eventually
and takes off into the bluest of skies on the
longest of days

There are foghorns out in space as well
warning against floating debris
the very air turning around inside air causes that
unmistakable crooning sound that accompanies
weightlessness

The predicament is we're all still here on and off the
telephone to Divine Reality Who's
always at home so it has to be trouble at our end
causing the bad connection static on the line gradual fadeout
or we haven't paid our bill for one flimsy reason or another

Yet the radiant sky is somehow itself proof of simplicity
and the calling across seeming emptiness by one
angel to another more gorgeously arrayed than an Amazonian Lyre-bird
should finally convince us the way
seemingly out of nowhere habitable cities arise
with their rainproof rooftops and intricate wiring
streets that lead to places up hills and into alleyways
oceans that unceasingly lap the shores around every land mass

seemingly perfectly happy babies becoming serial killers
seemingly perfectly miserable babies becoming ground-breaking
nuclear physicists
the enigma of it all only rarely slowing down enough to
take account of its anomalies

Daniel Abdal-Hayy Moore

But the heartbeat by God the heartbeat of us all
more predictable than the seasons
whose gyrations are more tumultuous than a beehive when a hornet's
wandered in
more prone to foolishness than a
so-called Third World country's revolutionary government
sorting out its priorities

Still the predicament from here is chugging puffs of
steam making lovely
whispery motions through the air like a loosely woven fabric so subtle
it actually
dematerializes as it unfolds
which seems to be the same for our lives
growing less and less substantial physically and more and more
identifiable inwardly as either

one who becomes a happy butterfly thoroughly awakened in the dream
or a drunkenly dreaming butterfly thinking it's awake but is actually

fluttering smoke in an updraft
scattering its precious wing-dust in the wind

Daniel Abdal-Hayy Moore

The Practice of Ecstasy

The tea refused to stay in its cup
floating in the air like a dark sunrise

The space in the door refused to stay in its frame
and walked out around various people and things
providing a clear way *through*

Little buttons refused to stay up and down a lapel
and formed curlicue designs on the side plackets instead

A general ecstasy took over
no one refused its invitation to drop their usual
concerns they unstrapped them unhooked them unleashed their
terrible tigers let their harnesses go so the fiery
stallions of their usual concerns could run free

The light refused to stay put in its place and visited
everyone's eyes one by one and collectively

The wind refused to go in just one direction and so it
blew up from beneath and out from inside and
from the top down enough to loosen the hinges of
everyone's preconceptions

We strode out for the first time unencumbered with fixed
prejudices

Daniel Abdal-Hayy Moore

A sound was purely itself in the great orchestral
swell of things
voices part of the ongoing saga from the
beginning of time to the present and
tunneling forward

Little tiny things refused to be overlooked and joined in the
general celebration

A shout went up in the air and continued
ascending

A blue ray fell through its center and turned it
into song

Daniel Abdal-Hayy Moore

Love Beast

Strike a gong! The love-beast has
returned with his

pelt of conquests around his waist
and Oh! how we long to be among them!

No tunnel that narrows at the end to a
black door with only nothingness beyond

no shriek of tragic circumstances or event
however definitive and life-changing

no tsunami dark Punjabi swami however
fierce and calamitous with glowering eyebrows

can stop the love-beast in his tracks
or trap him in however velveteen a trap

But he moves on through thick and thin
touching with a deft touch through
layer after layer the dormant heart
within

And each of us so touched displays a
curious fanning as of shutters of light and
dark almost falling open at that
astounding passage

And he smiles at himself in our own
faces that have now become mirrors for him to
smile in

Daniel Abdal-Hayy Moore

And he laughs to himself at all our trembles and
bumbles and treble clef bawlings and bellows
until they all become reverberant
echoes of his laughter in an equally dazzling
hall of mirrors in which His Face alone
shows

And he is deft and svelte and swells to
enormous size though thinner than a
hair

And rushes like a river through our pulses
until our hearts become his reservoir

And we fall over falls in his barrel
and barely survive with only an

empty barrel to show for it while he alone
reaps all the glory

Since he is the love-beast and we aren't
even his whiskers or hooves but only the
tap tap tap of where he

deigns to come in so long as nothing else
is there inside to pen him in

Free in acting and desiring without the
least shred of action or desire

Daniel Abdal-Hayy Moore

Free in longing and arriving without there being
anything in any future to long for or
arrive at

except the dissolution in pure explosion of all
longing and arriving and as well all future
by his slightest chronological maneuver
as he pats our hearts in passing with a delicate
momentary feather-duster and

is gone
that sweet intangible
love-beast

who leaves us with only his
twin feet repeating those

delirious dance steps he took to
track us down

Gone now

Oh now completely
gone!
_____

(Mevlana Rumi's birthday)

Daniel Abdal-Hayy Moore

Born in 1940 in Oakland, California, **Daniel Abdal-Hayy Moore**'s first book of poems, *Dawn Visions*, was published by Lawrence Ferlinghetti of City Lights Books, San Francisco, in 1964, and the second in 1972, *Burnt Heart / Ode to the War Dead*. He created *The Floating Lotus Magic Opera Company* in Berkeley, California in the late 60s, and presented two major productions, *The Walls Are Running Blood*, and *Bliss Apocalypse*. He became a Sufi Muslim in 1970, performed the Hajj in 1972, and has lived and traveled throughout Morocco, Spain, Algeria and Nigeria, landing in California and publishing *The Desert is the Only Way Out*, and *Chronicles of Akhira* in the early 80s. Residing in Philadelphia since 1990, in 1996 he published *The Ramadan Sonnets (Jusoor / City Lights)*, and in 2002, The *Blind Beekeeper* (Jusoor/Syracuse University Press). He has edited *The Burdah of Shaykh Busiri*, translated by Shaykh Hamza Yusuf, and the poetry of Palestinian poet, Mahmoud Darwish, translated by Munir Akash. He is also widely published on the worldwide web and his own website and poetry blog: www.danielmoorepoetry.com, www.ecstaticxchange.wordpress.com. Moore has read his poetry at conferences in North Africa and Europe, and has been a two-time finalist of the Nazim Hikmet Poetry Prize in 2011 and 2012. *The Ecstatic Exchange Series* is bringing out the continuing body of his life work of poetry, of which he has thirty-two titles in print as of March, 2012.

Anna Lena Phillips

Unfinished Story

Before her brother lost his shoe in the pluff mud,
before they went crabbing with rotten chicken necks,
before her sister fell in the creek at the ditch-bank,
there was this: once, back of the school bus, my mother
read past her stop, till the end of the route. Slouched down,
her knees against the seat, a tunnel of story
enfolded her; she didn't notice her house
go past, or else it wasn't there. Then no one was left
in the bus but her and the nearly golden light
of Charleston afternoon glancing off brown
leather seats, dust motes she did not see. The driver
parked the bus, checked through the rows,
careful receptionist thumbing through emptied files,
searching for the errant slip of paper, the last to-do
of the day. *Little girl!* He called her back
to the evening, traced the finished route
down quiet streets. She watched from the clouded
window, crying. The book lay closed on her legs,
its name obscured by her crossed hands
so even when I ask her what it was called,
I cannot see the title: now the only story's
the ride home, made backward, infused with fear.
Her parents, where are they? They might be angry.
She is alone, the world's changed, nothing
has come true, and this is where
the story ends: before she reaches home.

Anna Lena Phillips

"I'm Going Back to North Carolina"
        —*Sheila Kay Adams*

Come home with me and kiss me in dappled shade
along the bikeway and creek where muscadine
curls over asphalt path and sewer line,
covering the surfaces humans have made.
Above us on the overpass, tar and gravel
car-scattered, but here blackberries ripen
in cool and speckled shadow, hard green knots
of cells, white shreds of flowers, and still vines travel,

leafing and leaning into sun, as we
lean into their shade. Three years back we rode
this passage in the dark, an edge in us
crowded with possible fruit, stippled with day.
We cycled through that margin, into a field
of lengthening afternoons, a surety

to last us years together and years apart
from Carolina. Now, held fast in our
habitual sun, we tilt southward, needing more—
the shifting light of woods-edge to remind us
of first uncertainty that, tended, turns
into a constant chaos we can inhabit,

make a home in. Let's walk as the wild
grape moves, with curving purpose, toward shade
and back to the shine of noon, breathing in
the saving scent of honeysuckle, jewelweed,
summer grasses and our sun-warmed hair—
dizzying our senses, pulling us toward
each other's verdant bodies, summoning
a salve, a word to keep us: we live here.

Anna Lena Phillips

"Hand Me Down My Walking Cane"
—*Ralph Blizard and the New Southern Ramblers*

Pull the back door shut and drop the latch.
Hand me down my walking cane. I won't look back.

Rosin up the bow for one more tune.
How can I play this refrain and not look back?

You catch a glimpse or two; he steals them away—
keep hold of what you can, and don't look back.

I've done it all my life—kept misery
at bay with one firm line: Don't look back.

Anybody asks you where I've gone
say I've left on the midnight train and won't look back.

Look neither back nor forward—that's the way
to move. Drink up your wine, and don't look back.

Is that you, standing just beyond the porch light?
Well, step in out of the rain, and don't look back.

Anna Lena Phillips

Anna Lena Phillips was raised in upstate South Carolina and now lives in Piedmont, North Carolina, where she writes, edits, calls square dances, and serves as poetry editor of *Fringe magazine* (http://fringemagazine. org). Her poems appear in *BlazeVOX*, *International Poetry Review*, *Open Letters Monthly*, and the *Anthology of Appalachian Writers*, among others. A recipient of the Dorothy Sargent Rosenberg Prize for poetry and an emerging artist grant from the Durham Arts Council, she is at work on a project that investigates the ways we interact with computers, as well as the Endearments, a series of anagrammatically derived poems, documented at http://theendearments.wordpress.com.

Iris Tillman

Genealogy

1. Stories

What is lost may not be forgotten.
Listen, whispers rise like rumors
from sealed mouths.
Maps of bulldozed lands tear at touch,
their borders mangled like limbs.

(Some dug their own graves. Others stood at the edge and fell.)

The brain lights up, old tales glow like fires in ashes.
Watch out, they will sear your skin. More light, a voice cries.
This piece of skull marks an ancestor who walked
not where you walk now over roots near a park stream.
Life's easy on this side of family history.

Think of a hand offered.
Think of a boy so badly scalded
that he must die where he played
close by a hearth because an iron pot
tumbled its devastation on him
while outside the small house,
a hundred yards off, his mother
negotiates with a gentile officer
who has reached for her hand.
She's brazen, refuses to touch him,
tucks hers into apron pockets and waits.

The miracle is his turning away
from her wide, pretty face and lush braids.

Iris Tillman

The rough chimney smokes up the sky.
Clouds stiffen into peaks in the cold.
At the door she hesitates as though she knows
she will find her three-year-old, silent and bruised.
The floor steams around him.
Boiling water is his glistening shroud.

Too imprecise: Say the house was dirty and grew
like a diseased tree in the vicinity of *Kamenets Podolski*,
a region and town, a name with many variants.
Or it was a village of even more slippery nomenclature
like *Novayya Ushitsa*. Another prospect, far different
but also nearby, is *Minkovitz*, possibly mistaken
in passage for *Mischowitz* -- all out of tune, these shtetls,
chords of dissonance on displaced tongues.

2. Inheritance

Or you may remember the loss without having known
the presence like a story not handed down
like grandfather Smiel who became
Sam and disappeared into a single image
of a man with squinting eyes almost
washed out in the sunlight circling his head
like a halo where he sits and smokes
on a wooden chair in a white shirt
and you watch the curves of his eyelids
change into slants so delicate and strong
that their shadows deepen and tell
of horses and Mongols galloping across Russia
leaving their marks in the bodies of women.

Iris Tillman

Passover, 1952

To get to the Seder you must drive over roads
men travel to reach day jobs far from their suburban homes --
each morning's exodus unlike the one you celebrate tonight
at your aunt's dining room table where your uncle recites
the blessed sounds, *Baruch Atoi Adonoi.*

Women in the kitchen chop bitter herbs.
Sweet wine speaks of loss.
Anonymous souls haunt hallways.
Their scent is gas. History
disturbs the air with its ashes.
Like ghosts stacked on old carpet
the dead are everywhere.
They watch the small children shift,
uncomfortable in their stiff-backed chairs.
Their father intones the Hebrew prayer.

Little Miriam turns pages inked in red and gold,
follows the movements of her uncle's hands.
He holds the Haggadah and nods, even smiles at her.
She whispers words she can't understand.
Under the white tablecloth cousins pinch and kick.
Someone cries and then quiet descends among the chosen
who are grateful this night for God's blessing
even though it brings ten plagues upon the Egyptians.
No need to mourn their dead first-born.

Iris Tillman

You dip your fingers in wine.
You listen for the separation of waters.
You feel in muscle and bone the million steps in desert sand.
You are not sure what freedom is, but this year, Miriam,
you ask the question because this year you are the youngest of all.

Clean-shaven Uncle Morris in his white satin yarmulka
turns to the youngest boy, and you hear Aaron asking,
Why is this night unlike all other nights?
Rage grabs your heart at the injustice.

Iris Tillman

Mr. Blumenthal's Library
Wildacres, North Carolina

The open windows of this wood paneled room
give voice to bird calls, chattering squirrels, and wind,
which without the snap of trees would be silent
like the books on these shelves, leaning into each other
as if conversing, one *Arguing with God*
beside *The Language of Judaism;*
another exhibiting the *Guardians of our Heritage.*
In pale foil letters on a yellowing spine, I make out
God was in this Place although I've yet to see Him, or Her,
the last a sacrilege ten steps from *The Code of Jewish Law.*

At dawn in a Lower East Side tenement
my mother's father and brothers prayed,
their arms and heads bound by leather straps,
a small black box of miracles at each forehead.
Their bodies rocked back and forth
in a rhythm only they heard.
Their mouths moved without sound
while my mother watched, drawing
her own conclusions about the Almighty.

In those days my mother would parade down Hester Street,
wearing her best dress, pretending she was uptown,
but wherever she turned she heard the babble of voices,
multitudes of believers fervent in disagreement,
and she decided because there were so many gods
not even one could be true.

Iris Tillman

Her father never noticed the change in his youngest daughter,
who had survived influenza by a hair's breath the year before
and unlike her brothers at age thirteen had nothing to shed
when she walked away from God.

Iris Tillman grew up in Brooklyn, NY. From the age of five she studied ballet but gave it up at eighteen to attend Smith College where she began writing poetry and won a couple of poetry prizes. She wrote her undergraduate thesis on Shakespeare's sonnets. She got an MA in English from Brown and then left academe for scholarly publishing. In 1989 she helped start the Center for Documentary Studies at Duke University (CDS) as its Executive Director. Currently she coedits *Documentary Arts and Culture*, a book series published by CDS and the University of North Carolina Press. A few years ago she returned to writing poetry in her semi-retirement from her day job, and has benefited from the resources for poets in North Carolina, especially the encouragement of her writing groups and the generosity of poets who teach workshops. Her poems have appeared in the fall 2011 issue of *Tar River Poetry* and the first issue of the online journal *drafthorse/a lit journal of work and no work*. Several of her poems are forthcoming in *Women's Studies: An Interdisciplinary Journal* and in *and Love, a poetry anthology* to be published by Jacar Press. She lives in Chapel Hill, NC.

Tim Van Dyke

It is Night, But Within It is Luminous Day

Within the heated imagination of an inflamed desire—
a vision of God—
the trophy in some intimate and devastating plot,
the object of a spiritual abduction—
that the highest conceivable enjoyment lies in being loved—
to have death taste like bread and earth and the sea
to have one's sex be inscribed in the spurt of blood
anarchistically hailed by a barrage of poisonous vipers
encircling the face of a superficial pock
To poetize oneself into a young girl again
as an indirect reverberation will poetize a hypnosis,
a psychic mirror in which one is reflected
without awareness, under a different gaze—
Eyes close, and it is night; but within it is luminous day—
Within, the obliquity of a dream
one that traverses the universe in a single diagonal,
in order to touch the unknown blind spot,
the secret that lies sealed, the enigma
that constitutes the gaze, even unto itself—
a gaze that is marked out, that shall be run down—
To keep one's distance from it, to put off, to disenchant and deceive—
The lion's face engages a fate that must be completely free
as the girl must also be completely free
and in their freedom must reach out toward their own fall—
"to the zenith, dust of milk, a noon is with me"
and a strict sky of lawlessness hunches over
the electric divinations of children mired
beneath the supreme archways crisscrossing vaginal abysses
still mute with murderous energies trampling the thick of the land—
That the girl's fascination is exorcised, of a mythical figure,
an enigmatic partner, a protagonist in the liturgy,

Tim VanDyke

for seduction proceeds by absence; it invents a curved space
where the signs are deflected from their trajectory, their destination—
in this the lion's face lives without understanding, deprived
of every reaction, muzzled, circumvented
as a nothingness, as emptiness—
the final moment before passion's illumination—
for it is here, in nullity, in the absence,
in the mirror's face, that its triumph is assured—
that stroke that ties a movement
of the soul to its destiny and its unmarked grave

Tim VanDyke

The Ludic is Everywhere

Behind the screen of an ecstatic refraction
there is no longer any play—
no stakes, illusions, no representations
simply a matter of modulating the code
playing with it as one plays
with the tonalities and timbres of a stereo system—
No more Transgression, no more Transcendence—
Seduction in its radical sense: as dual, ritual, agonistic,
replaced by the seduction of an ambience,
the playful eroticism of a world without stakes
the cybernetic absorption of play into the Ludic
the polemic that organizes the space of the Law
the digitality of the signal, the polarity of the sign
that we are living in a supple, curved universe
that no longer has any vanishing points—
The lion's face outside the domain of pointless science
The lion's face swallowing islands like pennies
The lion's face formed of the play of a ritual
The lion's face formed of that past, cruel order,
where the risks were never ending and the stakes absolute—
The Ludic formed of sheer aimlessness
The Ludic formed of the play of the Model
against the demand for the Game—
but even as transgression, spontaneity, or aesthetic distance,
play remains only a sublimated form of the old pedagogy
that gives it a meaning, assigns it an end,
and thereby purges it of its power to seduce—
one can no longer speak of a sphere of enchantment
one no longer speaks of seduction
instead, an era of fascination begins—
The lion's face an amnesiac

Tim VanDyke

the amnesia consummated
in retrogressive fashion
raised to mass dimensions
The lion's face of forgetfulness, liquidation,
an annihilation of memory and history,
the same recessive irradiation, the same
echoless absorption, the same black hole
as Auschwitz—
an extermination that would then be deployed,
dissuaded by death, dissuaded unto death—
The lion's face a postmortem emotion
a tactile shudder that will enable them
to let the catastrophe slip into oblivion

Tim VanDyke

He Who is Not Painted is Stupid

The body is covered with appearances—
illusions, traps, animals and sacrifice—
what Artaud termed metaphysical—
a sacrificial challenge to the world to exist
for nothing exists naturally
things exist because challenged
and because summoned to respond to that challenge—
The lion's face springs forth two long ganglia, whirls and turns,
mourning the late sweet chord—
Not a simple appearance nor a pure absence
but the eclipse of a presence—
a prism of another space, a refraction,
a flickering, a hypnotic mechanism that crystallizes attention—
The lion's face undoes them all by making of itself a shimmer
a reworking of the body
to provoke and deceive Desire
to burn for a moment and then flame out—
as if to say, "Tell me who I am"
when one is indifferent to what one is
when one is a blank, without age or history—
a gesture that creates a unity in the texture and color of the skin
effacing the eyes behind more beautiful eyes
cancelling the lips behind more beautiful lips—
to be attentive to one's body, to care for and paint it
to set oneself up as a rival of God in an ostentatious ceremony,
the signs gravitating irresistibly around each other
so as to reproduce themselves
as if by magnetic recurrence—
that face— a dizziness,
a loss of meaning, a sealing of an indestructible pact
where all resemblances have vanished—

Tim VanDyke

rituals, masks, designs, mutilations, torture—
all to seduce the gods, the spirits, the dead—
absorbing all expression within its own surface,
without a trace of blood
so that death itself shines from its absence and insurgent cruelty,
the unspeakable cruelty of silence and its outrageous calculation

Tim VanDyke grew up in Colombia, South America, until guerilla warfare forced him back to the United States. Since then, he has worked in several insane asylums. His first book, *Topographies Drawn with a Divine Chain of Birds*, is out from Lavender Ink (2011). He also recently released a chapbook, *Fugue Engine*, with Cannibal Books. His work has appeared in *Fascicle*, *Typo*, *Octopus Magazine* and elsewhere.

Honorable Mentions

(In alphabetical order)

Elizabeth Gargano

Reflections

Clouds litter the gravel road
to our house, drifting in the standing
pools from last night's storm.
Inverted trees float there too,
black and jagged as cracks in a mirror.

The light's all wrong.
Half the sky's white as sheet lightning,
the other gray and soggy with rain.
Tunneling though a floating
slab of sunlight, a flutter of rust
charges my windshield.

I brake, feel the impact, a throttling
sound. I have to get out and peel it
from the glass, the robin's body
smashed by its own speed, the stiff
gray wings, the cupped, rose-petal chest,
still warm. I lay it off the road,
on a rise of grass, venomous green.
Behind it a rash of toadstools,
fat and sudden, flares like wreckage,
bloated in all that rain.

Elizabeth Gargano

That Summer

Emerald green, the snakes slipped out of the woods
behind our house, first two or three, ten, twelve,
then so many that the green hill rippled like the sea,
scales undulating through swaying blades
of grass. We left our cramped, boxy living room,
the twin fans spinning to chill the hot still air, and stood
on the steps in ninety degree heat. The snakes gleamed
in the sweat of the afternoon. Two twined together,
braceleting each other in an ancient courtship,
a third joined the mating, then more, until the earth
pulsed and throbbed in an orgy of free love, a utopia
of snakes where *loneliness* seemed an impossible word.

That summer a child had knitted our bodies together,
combining your chin, my eyes, in a strange new patchwork
of silky flesh. Our son's arms twined around my neck
like a heavy locket. He rode my hip as I brewed coffee
to keep awake, or stirred vegetable soup in a pan, my spoon
cutting a glistening orange trail as the carrots melted,
the tomatoes dissolved out of their skins. I lived in a cloud
of sweat, milk, and the sweet haystack smell
of baby-fine hair. Every morning you escaped

Elizabeth Gargano

to your office in town, barricaded behind stacks
of papers, away from the heat, the smells of singed soup
and strong coffee that settled over us like a warm blanket.
Our son cried in the heat, the crib, the bassinette,
happy only when holding onto us. That summer
whole countries sprang up around us. Box elders clustered
on the siding of our tiny house, crows dive-bombed
our garden, snakes surged in the grass. That summer,
whole countries sprang up between us, marking
the shifting borders under our feet. New shadows
ringed our fingertips when we touched.

Elizabeth Gargano

Harvest

One morning the crows settled
on the corn in the garden,
dark flames on the candled stalks.

I planted a broom in the earth,
straw end up, wrapped it in an old
raincoat, topped with a baseball cap.
That's when the caws turned to laughter.
They knew that trick.

Nothing to do but to practice
being a human scarecrow
waving the broom in impotent circles
like a witch who's forgotten the spell
to lift off, her baseball cap slipping
over one eye, her raincoat trailing
in the grass, rooted in the earth.

Elizabeth Gargano

Elizabeth Gargano has published fiction in *The Long Story*, *Iris*, *The Willow Review*, and *Women's Words*, and poetry in *The Pittsburgh Quarterly*, *Prairie Schooner*, and *Poem*, among other journals. She is the recipient of a Pennsylvania Council on the Arts Award in Fiction. She currently teaches at the University of North Carolina at Charlotte.

Emily Romeyn

Five Slices
of Edvard Munch's *The Scream*

As a girl without shoes,
I feel the smooth warm grain
Of the grey ply wood
Nail-sewn into a footpath
For the wanderers of soul and sport
Along the slick slice of water
On Oslo Harbor.

Red-smoothed orange-layered
Lacquer dusted hazel-dripping
Green melting blue-churning
Sky
An Eye
Too long un-blinked,
Staring down from the up-there
With its bloody iris
And make-up muddled tears
Gives me a devilish wink.
My own eyes bat their lids.

The boardwalk border of the
Bay shoulder shrugs lazily as
The wind expels dead air
Under its gray ply-pieces.
Sag, drag, swish, sigh.
So tics the tide
On its languid evening crawl
Toward this boardwalk slide
Where the souls and sporters
Seek their dusk-break thoughts.
Grand, beautiful, sinister.

Emily Romeyn

Space ripples ahead of me,
A smoke wisp curling up
From the underbelly boardwalk—
A hell-bound outpost,
A wilted streetman's fire?
No—it floats. It writhes!
Slitting the
Air with rips of
White-hot throat
Burning shrieking
The sky ripples
As my chest clamps
Closed, the air drips blood with
Each new wave of
Coursing
Burning
Skin-peeling wood-curling
Skirk-singing bleating.

A white sliver of light
Slides its body like a dancer
Rather moving in the night
Like a fluke pulled out of water
On the boardwalk stretched
In front of me
On the boardwalk stretched
Across the collar
Of Oslo Harbor.
On the boardwalk grey slates
I share footing with the image
Of a devil's curdled dream.

Emily Romeyn

Resighted

Wrenched from the black bodymold of a dream
I awoke in a curl, hands clasped behind me.
My lids peeled back and the bulbs in their casts
Smoothly reeled, taking in the black room's mask.

With a pop the right sphere squeezed from its holding
And perched warm and damp on the ledge of my face.
From its side itched two amber-petaled silk wings
That tested the air as they lapped at the breeze

From my open window the eye caught a gust
And slipped into flight, traced the moon's lit string;
It flirted and dipped on the black buoyant night
Unbound from my thoughts, my direction, my sight.

The connection was dim though a channel remained
So through my mind flickered the eye's solo flight—

An elephant's walk, a shell in the sand—
Without preconception the image is clean.
Nameless and empty of mind-mediation,
The winged eye sees from a water-skinned womb:

Four towers tremble and crunch at their centers
They sway as they lift and then pound to the ground.
A fat wrinkled bubble of grey swells above them,
It bellows and sways with the pillars' stiff march.

Emily Romeyn

A crystalline palm cradles light in its curve
Which blushes like skin, though bloodless and cool.
Grooved and submerged in an dull dimpled surface,
It catches the roar of a distant blue pool.

Return to me pearl of cloudless perception
Give me your wings and I give you my word—

Emily Romeyn, originally from Wisconsin, is a Junior English major at Davidson College in North Carolina. Within her English major Emily focuses on composing and critically examining ekphrasis poetry--poetry about art--and is fascinated by verbal/visual artistic combinations. Besides writing poetry, Emily enjoys creating visual art, especially pen ink illustrations.

Chapbooks of Previous Festivals
(available at www.amazon.com)

A chapbook of talks and poetry

First Annual Nâzım Hikmet Poetry Festival

April 19, 2009 • Raleigh, NC

Contributors

Invited Talks

Nâzım Hikmet: Harbinger of Hope
Dr. Greg Dawes

Nâzım Hikmet and the Poetry of Confinement
Dr. Erdağ Göknar

Finalists of the Poetry Competition
Judy Light Ayyildiz
Katherine Barnes
Jeffery Beam
David Need
Pamela Richardson
Christopher Salerno
Tony Tost
Chris Vitiello

Honorable Mentions
Mimi Herman
Güney Acıpayamlı

Poetry Selection Committee
Katherine Stripling Byer
Greg Dawes
Joseph Donahue
Hatice Örün Öztürk
Jon Thompson

A chapbook of talks and poetry

2nd Annual NAZIM HIKMET POETRY FESTIVAL

April 18, 2010 • Cary, NC

Contributors

Invited Talks
Nâzım Hikmet: The Forms of Exile— Dr. Mutlu Konuk Blasing
Brown University

Poetry Competition Finalists
Kamal Ayyıldız
Mel Kenne C.P. Mangel
George McKim
Scott Rudd
Anya Russian
Celisa Steele
Garrison Somers
Carolyn Beard Whitlow
Loftin Wilson

Poetry Selection Committee
Katherine Stripling Byer
Greg Dawes
Joseph Donahue
Jaki Shelton-Green
Hatice Örün Öztürk

A chapbook of talks and poetry

Third Annual
Nâzım Hikmet Poetry Festival

April 17, 2011 - Cary, NC

Contributors

Invited Talk
Eda: Intimations from Turkish Poetry - Murat Nemet-Nejat

Poetry Competition Finalists
Edwina Attlee
Michael Beadle
Kevin Boyle
Alicia Brandewie
Aaron Counts
Ansel Elkins
Terri Kirby Erickson
Daniel Abdal-Hayy Moore
Adnan Onart
Glenis Redmond
Maureen Sherbondy

Honorable Mentions
Alisha Gard
Maria Rouphail
Dianne Timblin

Poetry Selection Committee
Greg Dawes
Joseph Donahue
Dorianne Laux
Hatice Örün Öztürk
Jaki Shelton-Green
Jon Thompson

Made in the USA
Charleston, SC
23 April 2012